CHASE THAT SMILE

CHASE THAT SMILE

Approaching Midlife: a Marathon, Mount Kilimanjaro and an Ironman Triathlon

Harold Cabrera

Copyright © 2022 Harold Cabrera
www.chasethatsmile.com

The moral right of the author has been asserted.

Apart from any fair dealing for the purposes of research or private study, or criticism or review, as permitted under the Copyright, Designs and Patents Act 1988, this publication may only be reproduced, stored or transmitted, in any form or by any means, with the prior permission in writing of the publishers, or in the case of reprographic reproduction in accordance with the terms of licences issued by the Copyright Licensing Agency. Enquiries concerning reproduction outside those terms should be sent to the publishers.

Matador
Unit E2 Airfield Business Park,
Harrison Road, Market Harborough,
Leicestershire. LE16 7UL
Tel: 0116 2792999
Email: books@troubador.co.uk
Web: www.troubador.co.uk/matador
Twitter: @matadorbooks

ISBN 978 1803130 750

British Library Cataloguing in Publication Data.
A catalogue record for this book is available from the British Library.

Printed and bound in Great Britain by 4edge Limited
Typeset in 11pt Minion Pro by Troubador Publishing Ltd, Leicester, UK

Matador is an imprint of Troubador Publishing Ltd

Front cover designed by Hannah Poppe

To Tania, Sofia and Elisa
Let's continue to chase that smile
Love you lots!

Life is good. Thank you, thank you, thank you.

PROLOGUE

January 2013

I read an email from one of my best friends. The subject line was '*Revelation*, A Visual Poem'. It linked to a Vimeo video[1] by Sébastien Montaz-Rosset, with a quote from a poem:

> *The heat and the softness of the sunshine.*
> *The peace and the rawness of the storms and the cold.*
> *The motion and the rhythm and the ebb and flow of the tides and the wind.*
> *Of this glorious weather all around.*
> Revelation by Charlotte Davies

I watched the video and felt inspired by its powerful, exciting and beautiful visuals, along with a hypnotic voice bringing the poem to life. I replied:

Kyle, this is a perfect segue into what I've wanted to write for the past few days.

---

1   *Revelation*, a Visual Poem by Sébastien Montaz-Rosset: https://vimeo.com/57370112

I've decided that before the end of the year of my fortieth birthday, I want to have climbed Mount Kilimanjaro!

I know a few people who have attempted it, and it is doable for most. Tania and I are thinking of doing it together, but I thought I would extend the invitation to you and the rest of the guys. :-)

What do you think? I figured it's probably better than buying a Porsche for a midlife crisis. ;-) We have a few years to plan it and I know you can't predict what life will throw at you, but I think this is a nice goal to look forward to. I remember thinking about going to Sydney for the Olympics when we were at university, and that plan turned out pretty well. So I have a good feeling about this goal too!

Howie

October 2016

It was the off season, and I started thinking about races to do the following year. I wanted to run the London Marathon, but getting a place was impossible. A couple of people I know have done the Paris Marathon, and rate it highly. The Paris race takes place in April, around the same time as the London one. This meant that the springtime race shouldn't interfere with any others I ran in the summer. I looked at their website, and the cost was reasonable. On a whim, I tried registering to see if I could get a place, and, to my surprise, I did. I had thought it would be difficult to enter a big city marathon, but it turned out that wasn't so for Paris. That was it; I entered another marathon for the following year. Paris wouldn't be my first race of that distance, but it was probably the largest in terms of number of participants. I had grand plans for my fortieth year, and running a marathon was not a bad start. I thought that, even if I didn't do anything else when I turned forty, completing the Paris Marathon would be an achievement in itself.

November 2016

I read an article in a triathlon magazine which said that one way to get over the off-season winter blues is to book your races for the following year. I was thirty-nine, and the idea of doing an Ironman before turning forty kept popping into my head. I've been racing for several years but never attempted triathlon's longest race distance before. Swimming for 3.8 kilometres, then cycling 190 kilometres before running a 42.2-kilometre marathon seemed like an extremely daunting challenge. My stomach fluttered, just thinking about it.

Forty was just another number, but at the same time, it was a huge milestone. I would be reaching midlife, which could be the beginning of the dreaded midlife crisis. Well, at least I didn't have the urge to buy a fancy expensive car yet – signing up for a crazy physical challenge was way cheaper.

I did some research, and the Outlaw Triathlon in Nottingham was rated highly for beginners. It was a full-distance Ironman event with a mostly flat bike course on partially closed roads. The swim was in a rowing lake, which would be relatively calm, and the run seemed flat as well. I knew the event sold out every year, and that, if I waited any longer, I might not get a place. The Outlaw Triathlon was on 23 July; there would be enough time to recover from the marathon and complete the training for the Outlaw. It was a serious commitment, and I was nervous. Self-doubt flooded in, but at the same time, I was excited as I imagined myself crossing the finish line. That was when I knew I had to do it. I took the plunge and signed up, and soon afterwards the excitement overcame my nerves, reassuring me that I'd made the right decision. Whether I would finish the race was another story, but I looked forward to my first Ironman journey.

December 2016

Several weeks had passed since I'd booked the Outlaw, and the deadline to change my mind and get a full refund had come and gone. By December, my attention was focused on researching climbing Kilimanjaro. I'd been thinking about it for several years, ever since I'd heard someone climbing it for charity on the radio. I hadn't climbed any mountains before, and I wanted to try a new experience before turning forty. I read about the different routes, what time of year was best, what equipment was needed and which tour operator to use.

The first decision we needed to make was when to go. We narrowed it down to early June or early September. September was ideal for me because it would be after my Ironman and the climb wouldn't interfere with my training. Plus, my wife Tania and I both have our birthdays in September, and we could celebrate them on the mountain. However, our daughter Elisa would be starting primary school the following year, and we thought it would be unfair for her to start a new school without us around to support her. We planned to ask my parents – who live in Canada – to visit for a few weeks and look after the girls while we climbed the mountain. My parents are both retired, so their schedule was not an issue, but we thought it would be difficult for them to settle Elisa into school on their own. In the end, we decided June would be the best time to go.

According to my research, weather-wise, June was not a bad time to climb Kilimanjaro. It is the start of the dry season, so there would be less rain or snow. Plus, it wouldn't be the peak climbing season, so there would be fewer people on the mountain. The only problem was that it would be right in the middle of my

Ironman training. It wasn't ideal, but I reasoned that climbing a mountain was not exactly a walk in the park either, and a week-and-a-bit away from my training would be okay. We found a tour operator that would allow us to reschedule, if needed, up to a month before departure without any penalties. That sealed the deal and we booked our Kilimanjaro trip!

I didn't know what a midlife crisis looked like, but signing up for the Paris Marathon, climbing Mount Kilimanjaro and doing an Ironman triathlon sounded like one to me. I hoped I hadn't bitten off more than I could chew.

Wednesday, 11 January 2017

A couple of weeks had gone by since I'd started my training, and my fitness level was starting to pick up, albeit slowly. After Boxing Day, I did a couple of easy runs. I don't believe in New Year's resolutions, and I thought I might as well get some runs in before the year ended. But all that training was easily negated by the amount I drank during the New Year's Eve party we had at our house. A minor setback, but I quickly got back on it. I managed to do a fifteen-kilometre run on the 2nd of January, which was a good start to the year.

One of the best things that Tania and I did over the holidays was hiking. Since we'd booked our Kilimanjaro trip, we thought that it would be beneficial to do one hike each month. Mainly to test our equipment and break in our hiking boots – which were highly recommended by most websites and guidebooks that I read. Plus, hiking is something we enjoy a lot. We explored the Chiltern Hills, which are about an hour away from London – where we live – and so easily accessible to us. Granted, these climbs would be nothing compared to what we'd tackle on Kilimanjaro, but we figured it was better than nothing. Getting to spend a whole day with just the two of us, as well as being able to talk while we reconnected with nature, was what I loved about our walk. We called it our 'date hike', and I looked forward to doing it every month. I preferred our date hike to other couples' 'date night', but I wouldn't share it on Facebook.

I've been running for many years now, and what I enjoy most about it is the sense of relaxation I get by letting my mind wander – thinking of different ideas, reminiscing about past adventures or visualising future goals. I get such a buzz from this. During my run that day I came up with an exciting idea. I would chronicle my whole journey towards trying to complete the three massive challenges I had set for myself that year. I decided to jot down my thoughts during my training as a log of my adventure. I figured it would be interesting to look back at one day. I called Tania to meet her for lunch and excitedly told her about my idea. She loved it, and encouraged me to get started.

I was inspired, and committed to transcribing my thoughts while training for my crazy midlife challenges. I wondered what would come from this…

THE JOURNEY BEGINS

Tuesday, 24 January 2017

It was a slippery and foggy day, and I did an interval run to continue my marathon training plan. I had to run fast for a set period, followed by a slow recovery pace – a pattern which I repeated several times. Today I had to do three intervals of ten minutes each and then a two-minute recovery. I used to hate interval runs, perhaps because I was doing them wrong. Before, I thought that for each interval, I had to run at full pace, with my heart beating out of my chest and coughing up my lungs. Obviously, I could never sustain that for very long before collapsing.

    Eventually, I realised that I was supposed to do interval workouts by heart-rate zones. Using a heart-rate monitor for training is essential if you want to improve. Monitors are popular now, and there are cheap, basic watches available. I improved significantly when I figured out how to train with a monitor.

    Sports scientists have worked out the different training zones for optimal results. There are five zones, each corresponding to a different intensity based on a percentage of your heart rate. In Zone 1, the heart rate should be within 50–60% of maximum and the effort should be very comfortable, like warming up and cooling down. Zone 2 is within 60–70% of maximum, and the effort should be comfortable enough to hold a conversation. (The majority of long runs are here.) In Zone 3, the heart rate should be within 70–80% of maximum, and the effort should be moderate and breathing hard enough to be able to speak short, broken sentences. In Zone 4, the heart rate is at 80–90% of maximum. The effort is hard, the pace fast and breathing is forceful. Finally, in Zone 5, the heart rate is at 90–100% of maximum, and you're at full sprinting pace. It is unsustainable for long periods, and the breathing will be laboured.

I started training with a heart-rate monitor and, during interval runs, I go up to Zone 4, whereas before I would go all the way to Zone 5, which was a mistake. I enjoy intervals now because I imagine that each is like a mini race in itself. After going fast, I reward myself with a slow recovery period between sets and catch my breath.

When I saw the pavement was slippery with ice this morning, I figured the grass was the safer option. Growing up in Winnipeg made me an expert at walking on ice and snow. The trick is to do little shuffles as opposed to your normal stride. This makes everyone walk like penguins during the winter. However, running on ice is a completely different matter, and normally not smart.

While running, I remembered a book I'd read in which the author explained why we don't hear much about Japanese long-distance runners, even though Japan is the third-fastest marathon nation on earth after Kenya and Ethiopia. A difference the author discovered between the Kenyans and the Japanese is that Kenyans mostly train on dirt tracks, whereas the Japanese run on hard concrete pavements. The author believes this to be a major factor because the Japanese peak early and have shorter careers due to injuries. Today, I pictured myself as a slick, fast Kenyan gliding along the grass, with less chance of getting injured because of the softer earth. But in reality, the frozen ground felt harder than the pavement; plus the uneven surface made it difficult to find a steady rhythm. I was also scared of twisting my ankle. However, it was still a better option than the icy path and potentially landing flat on my ass.

Wednesday, 25 January 2017

I was supposed to do an easy recovery run today but decided to change it up and spend an hour on the turbo trainer – a great device for riding my bike indoors. I didn't have much time, so I took the turbo out from under the stairs, mounted my bike on it and set it up in my dining room. The turbo is a major time saver for triathletes, as I can easily get a solid workout in an hour without worrying about the weather or being hit by a lorry. Plus no red lights, or pedestrians to avoid.

Before hopping on, I spent about half an hour fitting a new set of clip-on aerobars to my bike. Aerobars are supposed to increase speed by making your position more aerodynamic, thereby reducing wind resistance. Keep in mind that when you're cycling your biggest enemy is the wind; well, that plus any slopes. Being aerodynamic is supposed to reduce my front profile against the wind and allow me to go faster. In the past, I could never sustain the aero 'tuck' position for long periods, probably because I bought the cheapest bars, and they didn't fit me very well. This time, I did more research and purchased a new set of bars that had a wide range of adjustments and allowed me to dial in the correct position. After a lot of fiddling around, I found one comfortable enough where I could sustain the effort without losing too much power or getting tired. I was pleased with the result, and completed most of my workout in the aero position. The slight problem was that, when I stood on the pedals, my knees hit the bars. The bike course for the triathlon is relatively flat though, so this shouldn't be an issue. I can't wait to see how they will handle on the road.

Currently my training is focused on the marathon, but in the back of my mind, I am more concerned about the triathlon. I've run two marathons before, but it will be my first Ironman. The Outlaw will be a journey into the unknown. The bike leg is the longest section out of the three disciplines. Therefore, I need to spend more time building my bike fitness. The tricky part is to get my body used to the workload without overtraining.

After my workout, I did a quick weigh-in and my weight dropped to 69.9 kilos! I'm very happy with that, considering that I've been well over seventy kilos since October. I usually aim for sixty-six kilos for my races, but in the past few years, I was lucky to hit sixty-seven. One of my main weaknesses is maintaining a proper diet, and the challenge is cooking a healthy meal that my daughters will eat. If I make something healthy, they usually won't touch it. Most of the time I stick something in the oven like chicken nuggets or fish fingers. Cooking two different meals is difficult, so I end up eating what they have. Plus, I have a bad habit of finishing their leftovers. Hence, weight control is an issue for me. This year I will try to make a conscious effort to eat healthily and perhaps even reach my target weight of sixty-six kilos. We shall see.

Thursday, 26 January 2017

What a cold start to the day. I was freezing in my light running gear when I did the daily school run. It was a bitter and windy five-minute walk to Sofia's school, and then another twenty-five minutes to Elisa's nursery. I wanted to save time by starting my run after I dropped off Elisa, but forgetting to check the temperature was a mistake. I couldn't feel my hands when I started running and it took me ages to warm up, but at least the pavement was not icy, so I didn't have to run on grass. Plus it was desirable to get used to the cold for Kilimanjaro.

The run itself was pleasant. My fitness level is improving, and I found it enjoyable. However, I was slightly concerned by my knees. I felt something last night when coming down the stairs. Not necessarily pain, but a light soreness. I've learned that it's important to listen to my body. My number-one rule is that if I feel any pain during training, I stop immediately, readjust, do stretches and then continue. If the pain persists, I cut the workout short and figure out what was causing it. During today's run, I was concentrating on my stride and how much my knees were absorbing the shock. They didn't bother me too much, but it was in the back of my mind the whole time. I suspect the problem was with the bike. I need to make some more adjustments to my riding position.

Last night, I put up my fundraising page. The idea came to me during one of my runs when I was visualising myself running the marathon leg of the triathlon. I do this a lot: use visualisation to keep me entertained while running. I was fantasising about doing the race, and thought that it would be cool if I asked all my friends to support me by doing some swimming, biking or running at the same time. Maybe they could throw a party with a paddling pool, a stationary bike and a treadmill so that they could take turns supporting me. Then I imagined that Tania could do a live-stream update of my progress so that they could cheer me on in real time. It would be cool if the video somehow went viral, and a lot of people started participating by doing a swim, cycle or run. Plus, if the video did go viral, it would be even better if I were supporting a charity. And that's how I decided to dedicate this year's challenges to a good cause.

In the past few years, several people I know had been affected by cancer. During my training for previous races, I would think about them and dedicate my swim, bike ride or run to them, in the hope that they would beat cancer and get better. Two of them had been fortunate and are in remission. But sadly my friend's dad passed away a couple of years ago, and last year my uncle also succumbed to the disease. My uncle loved running and had run marathons during his life. So I decided to do my challenges in memory of him, and to raise funds for Cancer Research.

I'd raised funds for Cancer Research in the past. But to be perfectly honest, I only did it so that I could gain entry to a race. At the time I felt a bit hypocritical because I was fundraising for purely selfish reasons. Plus, I don't like drawing attention to myself, so I didn't push the fundraising much. Although, I committed to cover the shortfall if I didn't make my target. That same year, I decided to enter another charity race, which was a sprint-distance triathlon. I thought it would help me to prepare for my first Olympic-distance triathlon, which was my main race for that year and the one I entered via Cancer Research. The thing that put me off with the charity race was that the organisers wouldn't let me participate unless I raised a specific amount of money. I explained that I was already fundraising for another charity through another event, and that most of my friends had already made donations towards that cause. I also offered another personal donation of £100 on top of the race-entry fee that I'd already paid. However, the organisers were strict, and I was shocked when they said that I couldn't race unless I met the minimum fundraising target. I thought that wasn't right, so I decided to forfeit my entry fee and not race. That experience left me with a sour taste regarding charity fundraising, and I decided that I wouldn't gain entry to a race via a charity place again. Don't get me wrong, I still support charities, and I believe that most play an important role. But I would rather donate to them directly instead of fundraising.

That was, until last night, when I put up my JustGiving page. This time I have a genuine reason to raise funds for Cancer Research. And I'm not doing it to gain entry to an event; I paid for my races months ago, and don't need to enter via a charity place. This time it will be different, and I have set a modest target of £1,000. As much as I don't like drawing attention to myself, I am determined to make an effort and hit this amount. I also decided that even if I don't reach my aim, I will personally make a donation and bridge the gap. But you never know; perhaps my fantasy of my challenge going viral will come true, and with luck I'll smash my fundraising goal and contribute to a worthy cause.

Saturday, 28 January 2017

Today I did bricks, and not the kind you use to build a wall. A brick session in triathlon means a bike ride followed by a run. I don't know why it's called a brick; probably because my legs are heavy like bricks after the bike ride. I looked it up, but couldn't find a definitive answer. It could refer to stacking one workout after another, like bricks in a wall. Or maybe it's an acronym: 'B' for 'bike', 'R' for 'run', and 'ICK' for how my legs feel until I get used to it. Or perhaps something more logical like 'bike, run in combination', plus a 'K' so it makes for a cool word. Who knows, but triathlon has a lot of jargon like this and, for the uninitiated, it's a minefield. Triathletes make up silly terms to make the sport sound cooler or themselves sound tougher. But this morning when I woke up I didn't feel tough; I was tired. I didn't get a good night's sleep due to my other half going out last night. I was up late waiting for her to get home, but then as soon as I drifted off, she came stumbling in and woke me up! It took me another hour to fall asleep. Typical.

It was still pitch black when I rolled out of bed at 6.30am, and I figured it would be safer and warmer to spin in my dining room instead of being outside. It's Parkrun today, so the turbo trainer made more sense. I pedalled lightly and paid attention to my knee. Thankfully, there were no problems there, and I had an enjoyable ride. As soon as it was over, I changed quickly into my running gear and was off to my local park, in time for the 9am Parkrun start.

Parkrun organises free, weekly five-kilometre timed runs around the world. They are open to everyone, and are safe and easy to take part in. Parkrun is excellent, and I'm glad that there's one at my local park, which is minutes from my door. Parkrun encourages people of every ability level to take part, and builds a community of regular runners. I met a lot of nice people through Parkrun, and look forward to seeing them every Saturday morning, rain or shine. The problem is, I find myself getting a bit competitive during these runs. I don't know why, but I can't seem to slow down when I am doing a Parkrun. Right now my training pace is around 5:40 minutes per kilometre (5:40/km). But with Parkrun, I normally run at under five minutes per kilometre. For me, this is a considerable jump in pace; even today, when I was consciously trying to slow down, my pace was still at 4:59/km. My watch was beeping at me the whole way, signalling that my heart was beating way past its threshold and if I didn't slow down it would probably burst out of my chest, like giving birth to H. R. Giger's Xenomorph in *Alien*. I know Parkrun is not a race – they purposely call it a run as opposed to a race – but with a lot of people running, it seems like a race, and I can't help but run full tilt. The cool thing about Parkrun is that you are timed every week, and they have stats of all your runs. I have this urge to run fast because in the back of my mind I don't want my average to go down. Also, I'm used to running with the same people going at a similar pace. I will run alongside, then try to pip them at the finish line. The five-kilometre distance is short enough that I could hold a fast pace the whole way around. But, today would be my last Parkrun for a while; the reason being that it doesn't fit with my training schedule and I am afraid that running at that pace will cause an injury. The speed work is beneficial for the marathon, but it doesn't help the Ironman. So today I ran fast and enjoyed racing a couple of guys, but for the next seven months I would just volunteer at Parkrun instead of running it.

Sunday, 29 January 2017

A tough run today. I couldn't get into a rhythm. It was probably due to a lack of sleep again, and yesterday's fast pace. Tania went to a friend's birthday party, and I was meant to go too. But we couldn't get a babysitter, so I elected to stay and look after the kids. To be honest, I didn't mind as I had a two-and-a-half-hour run scheduled for today. I figured I would get to bed early, avoid alcohol and get sufficient rest. Instead, I read until way past midnight, and was woken at 2am when Tania stumbled home. I tossed and turned for ages before drifting off again. In a blink, at the crack of dawn, Sofia roused me, beating my 6:30am alarm. Well, it wasn't exactly dawn because it was still pitch black outside, but the whole household was wide awake. I put my head under a pillow to get more shut-eye, but it was no use. That battle inside my head had already started. One voice was arguing that I should go back to sleep, enjoy the cosy bed and have a lie-in. And another voice saying that I might as well get up and start running. Back and forth it went, until I yelled at both voices to shut up and let me sleep!

The workout voice won, and I rolled out of bed, gaining a tiny victory. Yet, I know my body; I felt sluggish and tired. Going for a two-and-a-half-hour run on four hours' sleep is not an exciting prospect. But I recalled a training tip that I read somewhere; namely, 'however crappy you're feeling, you should always try to start a workout and give it at least ten minutes, then reassess. If you still feel like shit and mentally not into it, then it's probably best to turn around and rest'. This was sound advice, so I shovelled a bowl of porridge into my mouth while planning how much water and energy gel to bring. On my way out, I said goodbye to the girls, who were glued to their weekend cartoons, getting their fill on their allowed TV time. I reminded Sofia to be ready by the time I got back in about two hours and forty-five minutes, because we planned to go to church.

Tania and I are not overly religious. However, our daughter goes to a Catholic school, so we aim to make an appearance once in a while. We can't remember the last time we attended, so we probably should go today. It was 7.15am when I left, and I calculated that the route I'd planned would take me just under two-and-a-half hours. I had to stop for traffic and to refill my water bottle, which would add another ten minutes to the run. Plus, I usually finish my run at the park and walk home as part of my cool-down, so another ten minutes. It was going to be close to get back in time, have a shower and then walk to church for the 10.30am Mass. The pressure was on, but it was an appealing target, so it was 'challenge accepted'.

By the time I got out the door, the streetlamps were still on, the lights reflecting off the frosty pavement. I had enough layers on, so it wasn't exactly freezing, and within minutes I warmed up. The roads were empty with just the sound of my feet hitting the ground. My local park was peaceful, beautiful, with a thin strip of fog hovering over the field. I got going slowly, and it stayed that way. I couldn't get comfortable and settle into a rhythm. I perked up when the sun started to rise, and I saw the mosque by the Regent's Park Hanover Gate. As I entered the park, I got a boost seeing all the other runners already out, plus the usual peloton of cyclists zooming past. I planned to do two laps around the Regent's Park outer loop and then head back. The first lap was okay, but by the second fatigue started to set in, and I struggled. The energy gels helped, but I kept on stopping because of some niggle in my foot.

Eventually, I managed to push on and make my way back. Getting to church on time spurred me on. Not because I wanted to go, but because I would be disappointed to miss out on some family time. I know that training will take up a lot of my time, and I'm glad that Tania is extremely supportive and understanding. But one of my reasons for getting my workout done early in the morning is to minimise the time I spend away at the weekend, and to allow me to hang out with my family.

My watch read 9.55 as I reached my front door. This would be enough time to have a quick shower and make it to church; surely the girls would be ready and waiting for me by now? But as I walked in, I found them all still in their pyjamas! I couldn't believe it; I'd run twenty-four kilometres, and they'd just finished breakfast. But I couldn't say much because I'd been out for nearly three hours. All I could do was coax them and help the girls to get dressed, then have a quick shower and rush out the door. I was too tired to walk, so we took the car and made it to church just in time.

Monday, 30 January 2017

Waking up was hard today. Everything was sore, and I could barely move anything. Luckily, I managed to get to bed before ten last night and had a decent sleep. I was aiming to get a solid nine hours, but my plan was foiled by Sofia rousing us at 6am again! I angrily told her to stay in bed for another hour. It was too late, though, as my mind was awake, but my body still required more rest. The run yesterday has taken effect, and if I were following a normal marathon training schedule, today would be a rest day. However, as the marathon is only one aspect of the triathlon, I couldn't ignore the swim and bike parts, and I had a 2,500-metre swim as part of today's schedule. It was not an appealing prospect, but I consoled myself that it would be a slow recovery swim.

When I got to the pool, the usual people were in my lane, plus a newbie, who was too slow for that lane. The pool has three lanes: slow, medium and fast. I normally use the fast lane, as I think I'm fast enough to keep pace – not the fastest, but I'm aware enough to yield and wait for the faster swimmers at the turns if need be. However, some swimmers are completely clueless about the pace for any given lane, and end up blocking everyone else. This leads to 'lane rage' in the fast swimmers, and some will get angry enough to pass aggressively to send a message. Now, as I've said, I swam at a relaxed pace, but even so, the newbie was so frustratingly slow that I had to pass him several times. Eventually, he took the hint and moved lanes, and the tension dissipated from the faster swimmers.

Eventually, I settled in and was enjoying my swim, but then out of the corner of my eye, I noticed a person enter the lane on the other side. At the time I didn't think anything of it, until – bam! "What the f*@#?" I gurgled underwater. I looked up in confusion and realised that the person was swimming in the wrong direction! I tried not to get angry and gave the person the benefit of the doubt, assuming that he didn't know the rules. I calmly pointed to the sign and explained how it worked. The pool has clear signs at the end of each lane indicating the speed and the swimming direction so that swimmers can avoid collisions. Swimming in the wrong direction was even worse than swimming slowly because someone could get hurt. Hopefully, he wouldn't make the same mistake again.

After the collision, I lost my momentum and all of a sudden my body was like a dead weight. I cut my workout short and went even slower in the last set in order not to overdo it. This helped, and I enjoyed the relaxing sensation of the water. When I got out of the pool, I felt energised and ready to tackle the day. I'm glad that I'd managed to do the workout at all, considering my long run yesterday.

Tuesday, 31 January 2017

Today was a pleasant recovery run: thirty minutes of an easy, slow pace. It was drizzling, so not the best weather. A typical London winter's day, but at least it wasn't too cold. My legs were heavy when I started the run. It was obvious that the effort from last Sunday's long run was still having an effect. I decreased my pace even more and looked at my watch, which indicated around 6:25/km. This was pretty slow indeed, which brought to mind the pace that I would need to be running to achieve my goal of completing the Paris Marathon in under four hours.

Last year I ran the Manchester Marathon with a personal best of 3:58:43. However, it was only my second marathon, so I had been sure I was going to get a PB. Running under four hours is a major goal for most amateur runners and I've ticked that box, so for Paris this is not the main target. Having said that, I am still aiming to run this race at the same pace. Granted, Manchester is one of the flattest marathon courses in the world, so Paris might be tougher. Also, the weather is going to be key. Last year, a friend of mine ran his first Paris Marathon and by all accounts he was fitter and faster than me. But what he didn't consider was the hot weather, nor his race nutrition. He was aiming for three hours and fifty minutes, but ended up finishing over four-and-a-half hours. This goes to show that you can never discount the weather. Although, race experience accounts for a lot too, which may be why he didn't do too well with his race nutrition. This year, we're doing a swap. He's running the Manchester Marathon, and I'm doing Paris. We're exchanging notes, which will potentially help us both.

When I did the Manchester Marathon, I knew that to get under four hours, I would need a pace of around 5:35/km. Today, I doubted that I could get back to that level. The reason is that I had a look at my training runs from last year during the same period, and the long runs that I did exactly a year ago were bang on 5:35/km. My run last Sunday was at 5:55/km, which was concerning. At that pace, my predicted marathon finish would be 4:09:39. Still a respectable time, but way over four hours. Perhaps it was due to lack of sleep. I will have to see what happens with this Sunday's run.

The other thing that came to mind during today's run was the weird dream I had last night. I dreamt that I was somewhere in Paris, and I was lost in the Métro subway system. I kept going around and around different train platforms, and every time I tried to get out of the station, I kept popping up in some restaurant. After several tries, I eventually managed to get out to street level, where I watched the end of the marathon. I wasn't too disappointed, and even ended up cheering the runners, plus other stragglers who also seemed lost. I then went back down into the station and was astonished to find a banquet waiting for me, with some family and friends already eating. So I sat down and tucked in. I smiled during my run as I thought about the dream, as I don't have to be Freud to know what my subconscious was telling me. Obviously, I'm hungry!

Wednesday, 01 February 2017

The benefit of having a training programme to follow is that it eliminates most of the planning and thinking about what sessions to do. However, I find that some flexibility is necessary, especially as I'm combining a pure marathon training plan with an Ironman Foundation programme. That's right; the Ironman is so tough that you need a separate training programme to get into sufficient shape to start the real training. So today, I skipped the short intervals that the marathon session called for and hopped on the turbo for an hour instead. I also made some adjustment to the aerobars and saddle of my bike to see if the minor knee problem I experienced the other day would go away.

As usual, sleep was poor last night. The day started earlier than normal because it is Sofia's birthday. She was so excited that she couldn't sleep all night. She kept coming into our room on the hour, every hour from 2am until 6am, when we finally gave up, and turned on the lamp to start the day. As part of our tradition, I'd hidden all of her gifts around our room the night before. I was one step ahead and didn't do it in the living room, so that I could lie in bed a little longer while she searched. I drifted off soundly until she found all of them. The last present she opened was a book on positive thinking that I got her.

When I was growing up in the Philippines, we didn't have much. I wouldn't say we were lacking, but I guess from a Western standpoint we were. My parents still provided the basics such as clothes and food, and we went to a private school. However, private school in the Philippines is not the same as private school in the UK. Filipino private schools are only slightly better than the public schools there, so don't get any ideas that we're middle class or anything, because we were far from it. I had some toys, but mostly we played with the other kids around the neighbourhood – going for bike rides, kicking a ball on the street, playing hide-and-seek; that sort of thing. I used to watch a lot of TV when I could. We only had one TV, and it was always a fight with my brother and sister to see who got to watch something. When it was my turn to watch my shows, I used to watch a lot of American family sitcoms; the ones where every family is happy, and whatever dramas there were that week were always solved by the end of the half-hour episode. One of my favourites was *Full House*, and I fantasised that one day my life would be something like the show. Every time things weren't going my way, or if something was getting me down, I would fantasise about living in my version of *Full House*, having a cool car and living in a basement bedroom like Joey, one of the characters. Using my imagination to cheer myself up stayed with me as I was growing up, and looking back, I am sure this is how I developed my positive personality. I didn't realise it at the time, but after reading some self-help books as an adult I realised that I was practising some powerful positive thinking, manifestation, visualisation and mindfulness. I gained the knowledge that thoughts are real forces. From such a young age, I learned how to use my thoughts to control my emotions, motivate me and manifest my reality, which I guess some adults still don't know how to do. Even now, I use these techniques every day, especially when I'm training. I believe that this is what gets me through any task and allows me to finish all of my races. One of my goals, is to teach this method to my kids.

Tania made some special chocolate-chip pancakes for Sofia's birthday, which were delicious. It was probably not the best fuel for a workout, but it was difficult to say no to chocolate-chip pancakes. After dropping off the girls at school, I set up the turbo and made the adjustments to the bike. As soon as I got on, it was such an improvement. I found it interesting how a few millimetres of adjustment made such a difference. Most bike shops would say that it's important to have a proper fit for a bike. There are even bike-fitting companies that use specialised sensors and computer analysis to check you get the best position. I was considering getting fitted this year, but decided not to as I've already spent a small fortune on all the challenges that I'm doing. So I used YouTube instead and found a lot of helpful videos that showed me how to do it.

After the turbo session, my knees were better. I wish I could say the same for Tania. Since our last hike, she's come down with a bad chesty cough, a bladder infection and her lower back started acting up again. She had to take two days off work last week, and has been on antibiotics. It's a shame because she's doing well with her training, doing a lot of classes and strength training in preparation for Kilimanjaro. So last week has been a setback. Although, the bladder infection is now gone, but her cough is still around, and her back is not 100% yet. She's seeing a physio tomorrow, who hopefully will sort things out.

Thursday, 02 February 2017

That eight-hour sleep still eludes me. I went to bed early at 10.15pm, thinking that I would finally get a decent night's rest, only to be woken around 4.30am by painful heartburn. To top it off, Sofia woke up at the same time, saying she couldn't sleep. So she ended up sleeping in our bed, and I had to sleep in hers. Except I couldn't sleep because of the pain, and when I finally started to drift off it was time to wake up again. I need to sort out this lack of sleep, otherwise it will be detrimental to my training. I know it's my fault, for eating a lot at the restaurant last night for Sofia's birthday. I ordered sensibly and had grilled chicken with rice. The problem was that the girls ordered too much and I couldn't help finishing Elisa's burger and chips, plus Sofia's macaroni and cheese, and the rest of Tania's pitta bread with tzatziki – yum! Not to mention two or three sips of the girls' chocolate milkshakes, and Sofia's chocolate birthday cake. I was so full that I was already in pain before going to bed. So I only have myself to blame for my lack of self-control, which is a shame because I'm losing weight and getting healthier. But as they say, two steps forward and one step back.

It was warm today, so I took Elisa's scooter instead of her pushchair to drop her off at nursery. It's more work for me taking the scooter because Elisa will scoot about a hundred metres and then say she's tired, and I have to pull her all the way there, hunched sideways the whole time, and having a sore back by the time we get there. But she's getting too big for the buggy; plus it's healthy for her to get some exercise. It's always a battle of wills to get her to scoot, and there were tears today because she wanted to scoot across the road all by herself. So I stooped to her level and explained that she's still too little for the drivers to see her crossing, and therefore it's dangerous. I love her determination and independence, but there is a time and a place for them, and attempting to cross the street when she's three years old is not it. After the tears, and using all the tricks I had at my disposal (including distraction, reverse psychology and idle threats, amongst others), we eventually settled on me pulling her for a count of ten, and then her scooting while she counted to ten. A small sense of parental victory for me, and it had the bonus of getting her to count; apparently it improves a child's mathematical skills if they count something every day. Although, the victory was costly, as it took us fifteen minutes longer than the pushchair.

Luckily, my work schedule is flexible. I work as a consultant doing software development for a small company. The company has a number of stock and options trading strategies that we teach to our clients. I develop the back-end software algorithms that look for the trades. I love my job, because it's challenging but not stressful. I find it especially rewarding when we hear from users of our software that they've made money using our systems. The best part of my job is that I work from home, so I can work when it suits me, as long as I deliver. This allows me to do the school runs, look after the girls after school and make dinner every night. And, I can fit my training schedule around my work. This work-life balance is so important, and I am fortunate and extremely thankful to have it. The only downside to working from home is that I miss the social interaction you get from working in an office. I used to work for a big investment bank in the City; London's financial centre, where there is always a boozy social scene. A few pints at lunch is not uncommon, and going out for drinks after work is the standard. But missing this social aspect is a small price to pay for the flexibility of working from home. Not having to ride the cramped London Underground and smell some guy's armpit all the way to the office is enough reason to give it all up.

So even with the scooter drama and being late for the nursery, I didn't have to worry about getting my run in this morning. Today's session called for a forty-minute easy run. The weather was warm but windy, and the ground soggy. Nevertheless, I enjoyed it and I was rejuvenated when I finished; I was smiling, ready to start my workday.

Sunday, 05 February 2017

It's true when they say that if you do something for thirty days, it becomes a habit. Training today was automatic; I've been doing it long enough that it has become habitual. There was still that slight trepidation when I opened my eyes, but my body seems so used to it that doing a twenty-four-kilometre run almost seems normal. I took this as an encouraging sign, and I had more determination this morning, even though it was another six-hour sleep for me. When I walked out the door, the twilight and cold air felt refreshing.

I started my slow warm-up but immediately sensed some niggles in my right foot. I had to stop several times to readjust, and eventually the pain went away. Then I got going properly. My lungs expanded deeply, I wasn't tired and my form seemed okay. As I crested a small uphill section, the sun started to peek through, and its warm energy enveloped me. It made me remember when I went backpacking in Australia, right after graduating from university, with six of my uni friends. That trip was a pivotal point in my life. I learned so much about myself, and it shaped the person I am today. Before travelling to Australia, I had a preconceived notion of how my life would turn out. The goal was the engineering degree, then get the big job, the big house, the big car and the big TV. But during our Oz trip, I remember sitting on the beach with just the clothes on my back, my flip-flops and a stinky towel, and being completely content and happy. As most backpackers would say, we caught the travel bug pretty bad. I am lucky that, out of the seven guys who went out there, six of us are still great friends. We have formed such a tight friendship from that experience. Since going to Australia in 2000 for the Sydney Olympics, we've gone on other trips together, perhaps always seeking to recreate the incredible memories that we shared in Oz.

One such experience was going clubbing in Sydney's Kings Cross. That night I was with Slater, Kyle, Bruce, and Burton – Roz had already gone home, and the other friend we were with was slowly drifting away from the group. When we walked in the club it was still empty, but it had a cool atmosphere and the house music was quality, so we bought a drink. The repetitive upbeat tempo immediately grabbed me and I just started giving it on the empty dance floor without a care. I ripped it up pretty good, and when I was sufficiently tired, I found the guys chilling out in the corner as the place slowly filled up. I sat down and Kyle or Slater yelled in my ear saying that they'd just dropped some pills, and offered me one. I hesitated since I was an ecstasy virgin. But I reasoned that we'd been such close friends for years and travelling the last couple of months made that bond stronger. A montage of our recent adventures flashed through my head – I'm jumping out of an airplane over Lake Taupo, I'm bouncing upside down a cliff with a bungee cord attached to my legs, I'm paddling through grade 5 rapids in a raft, and I'm kissing a giant Maori wrasse underwater in the Great Barrier Reef – so I knew I didn't want to miss out. With a huge grin, I said yes, and he handed me a green pill with an apple on it. I popped it back, grabbed some water and went back to the dance floor. Initially, my body tried to reject it, and I almost threw up. But I held it in, and after about half an hour, sweat started pouring and as I ran my hands through my head, everything was tingly, I was floating in space, being spun around by the music, then the rush of euphoric energy surged through me, and I had no choice but to move every muscle of my body. I'd given the keys to the DJ, and he was fully in control. He was my puppeteer and I was his dancing marionette, connected to his turntables via musical strings. It was intense, and he had me most of the night.

While taking a breather in the chill-out room, I told the guys that our friendship was like *Voltron*, a cartoon I used to watch about five lions that join together to make a robot called Voltron, Defender of the Universe. I told them that I am the black lion, the body and head of the robot. Bruce was the blue lion, my right leg. My left leg was Burton, the yellow lion. Kyle was the green lion, my left arm; and red lion Slater, my right. I suppose the pill – like being stoned – had my imagination going and everything that came out of my mouth was pure genius (or shite depending on your point of view). To this day it's such a special occasion when the Voltron Force comes together. But sometimes while running, I see myself as a colourful robot with my friends in charge of moving my limbs and I'm just there for the ride.

As the music faded, I stumbled out into the Sydney twilight, which was soon replaced by the bright new day, excitedly telling everyone that I just had my first all-nighter. The other guys were exhausted and headed back to the hostel, but Bruce and I were still buzzing, so we started walking. We reached Hyde Park and sat on a bench to watch the sunrise. Chatting and reflecting on what we'd just experienced, imagining what the future would be for us, now that we'd finished university. Suddenly, the loud clang of church bells echoed in my ears and I looked behind to see a massive cathedral. I turned to Bruce and said that my Catholic mom was disappointed that I hadn't been to church in years, and dragged him up to head towards it. As soon as I stepped through the grand entrance, I was humbled by the gigantic, blindingly gorgeous space. After dipping my fingers in the holy water, and making the sign of the cross, we walked over to an empty pew. I welled up when I heard the choir singing, possibly due to the pill's residual effects. While I sat there, tears streaming down my face, I looked over to Bruce and saw him bobbing his head to the music as if the organ was playing some drum 'n' bass. I laughed hysterically, and saw the parishioners turn around with dirty looks. I then yanked Bruce out of his trance and told him it was time to get out, and hurriedly walked outside, sniggering. We headed back to the hostel, to wake the guys and check out Manly Beach. The day had just started.

Having my mind wander and remembering that moment back in Oz is why I love running. When I get into that zone, where my body goes on autopilot and my mind is free to wander off, small things will trigger memories that I can relive and cherish. Some people find running boring, but I'm the opposite. I find it completely relaxing and pleasurable because I get to replay these moments in my head. My brain made the connection between today's sunrise and the sunrise I experienced seventeen years ago, and brought me a huge smile. Just thinking about that time was enough to trigger the endorphins and give me that 'runner's high'. Perhaps my brain was recreating the feeling I got when I took that green apple pill many years ago.

Monday, 06 February 2017

My long run yesterday was both good and bad. Good because my pace picked up, but bad because I got a lot of tiny niggles in both feet throughout, and had to keep stopping to shake them out. Even though my pace of 5:44/km for twenty-four kilometres seemed okay, I realised that my body was getting tired and I needed to cut back this week to let it rest. Last night, I decided to rest for two full days including today. However, I changed my mind and figured that I would do a slow recovery swim instead and see how it goes.

When I got to the pool, it was quiet, and there were only two other people in the water. This was perfect because I could take it extra slow and not worry about keeping up a certain pace in my lane. But as soon as I got in the water, everything felt heavy. My legs would barely move, my breathing was laboured and there was a kink in my shoulder. I did my usual warm-up and willed my body to wake up. However, it never did. I was drained after a couple of laps, and my technique was suffering because I was compensating for my weary legs and weird shoulder. That was when I decided that it was best to call it a day and listen to my body. Sufficient rest, rather than doing some 'junk miles', was what I needed. The rule is that workouts should generally have a purpose, and junk miles are the ones that don't produce a specific physiological benefit. Continuing in my state would have been counterproductive.

In swimming, your technique is everything. When I realised that my form was not as it should be, I stopped right away, because I didn't want to imprint bad movements upon my muscles and develop bad habits. Therefore, aborting the swim was the best thing to do. As I've said, I find that it's important to listen to my body when training. I don't subscribe to the 'no pain, no gain' mentality. I think training should be enjoyable. For me, it's not just about getting the results, but also about enjoying the process along the way. Perhaps if more people approached exercise and training this way, they would stick with it longer.

Thursday, 09 February 2017

I had another weird dream last night. I dreamt that I was preparing for, or in, a race, and I was negotiating a tricky bike course. The course was on a mountain covered with boulders. Then, after riding some steep parts, we were on a ridge, and I could see large drops on both sides. The guy in front of me fell off his bike and dropped down about five metres. I stopped, reached out and tried hard to get him back up. I managed it eventually, but then I lost my grip on my bike, and it fell down the side of the mountain. I was upset, and then suddenly I found myself riding on a turbo, along with all the other riders. One guy came up to me and explained that if I somehow aligned my bike facing forward along the earth's orbital path with the rear wheel facing some non-existent comet, I would travel much further and gain time on everyone else. I struggled to figure out how this would work as we were all riding the stationary turbo trainer. Then the scene changed once more, and we were outside getting ready to ride the mountain again, but this time it was pitch black. So we had to put on our head torches, except I hadn't brought mine. Again, panic ensued, and I was left struggling to follow the rider in front of me, until we came to the same ridge and I realised that I couldn't see where I was going, and was going to fall. As I was about to plunge down the abyss, I woke myself up.

I looked at my watch; it was five in the morning. My mind was racing, and it would be hard to get back to sleep. I knew right away what my subconscious was thinking. Before going to bed, I did some research to find out if it's advisable to run a marathon before doing your first Ironman. Some people don't recommend it, but the consensus seems to be that it's okay as long as you give yourself sufficient time to recover. The general advice favours a minimum of four months between a marathon and a first attempt at an Ironman. The stress that a marathon puts on the body takes about two weeks to recover from; some even say four to six weeks. I knew from my marathon last year that it took me about ten days before I started training again, so I'm cutting it close between the marathon and the triathlon. Not to mention that I need about eleven days to climb Kilimanjaro.

Also, looking at my training data for last year, I know that because of the marathon, I did a lot less cycling during the build-up to the half-Ironman race that I did. This resulted in a slower time compared to the previous year, which got me slightly anxious about whether I would manage to complete the bike phase of the Ironman within the allotted cut-off time, let alone finish the whole distance. So when I woke up from my dream, it was pretty obvious why I'd dreamt it. I struggled to get back to sleep, because my mind was preoccupied with the bike leg of the triathlon. I wanted to look up how long it took me to ride a similar distance in the past; an urge which kept me awake most of the night.

Over breakfast, I talked to Tania about my concern regarding doing the marathon and completing the Ironman. This helped me to reassess my goals. My ideal would be to run the marathon in under four hours, then summit Kilimanjaro and finish the Ironman. After speaking with Tania, I realised that, out of the three targets, the first was the one I wouldn't mind not achieving, because I had already run a sub-four-hour marathon. It is more important to me to achieve my first Ironman, and this means that I have to re-evaluate my training. To date, I had been following a marathon training plan and adding some swimming and cycling. Given that the bike is the longest leg of the Ironman, I have to spend more time in the saddle, and should probably not worry too much about the speed-work sessions for the marathon. Since this will be my first Ironman distance, it's a journey into the unknown, which I'm sure is part of the cause of my anxiety. However, having reassessed my goals and discussed it with Tania, I was more optimistic. Maybe now the weird dreams will stop, and I will get some decent sleep again.

Of course, today's session would be another interval run. I decided beforehand that I shouldn't worry about going faster so that my body can cope better with the extra bike sessions. However, as soon as I started, I couldn't help going faster. The run was a breeze, and my body just kept wanting to push more during the intervals. Even though I was consciously trying to run slower, my body wasn't listening. It wanted to go fast and push hard. I figured that the extra rest was paying off and this was the result. So I just went with it and focused more on my body alignment and technique. In the end, the run was invigorating, even with the lack of sleep.

Saturday, 11 February 2017

It was particularly funny when Elisa asked me why I was going for a bike ride in the middle of the night. I told her it wasn't the middle of the night; it was 7am. When I looked outside, the streetlamps were still on, so my three-year-old had a point. But I didn't notice that it was snowing, so I didn't take my sunglasses, thinking that it was too dark to wear them and that the chances of the sun showing up were small. When I started off, there was very light flurries, then it started to get progressively heavier. I considered turning back but I was already too far away from my house. The wind picked up too, and the snow started pelting my eyes, so that I couldn't see. It was like going snowboarding without goggles in a blizzard; the normally harmless fluffy snowflakes hurt when they hit at speed. I rode with my head down and looked up once in a while, squinting as much as possible to protect my eyes and cursing myself for not bringing sunglasses. It was brutal, but I felt like a hardcore cyclist. I pictured myself tackling the *Passo di Gavia* in the 1988 Giro d'Italia.

The promising thing about today's ride was that I felt comfortable in my tuck aero position, and with the snow, it was like downhill skiing. Also, I didn't get any pain in my knees at all, and I was relaxed being down on the aerobars. The only problem was that I could hear the bars rattling when I wasn't leaning on them. I had to stop once and tighten all the screws, but it didn't help. It was annoying, and I broke Velominati's Rule #65.[2] The

---

2 *The Rules* by Velominati Keepers Of The Cog: http://www.velominati.com/the-rules/

Rules is a sacred text wherein lie the simple truths of cycling etiquette that all self-respecting road cyclists must follow. Rule #65 states that:

> *Bicycles must adhere to the Principle of Silence and as such must be meticulously maintained… No squeaks, creaks, or chain noise allowed. Only the soothing hum of your tires upon the tarmac and the rhythm of your breathing may be audible when riding.*

Clearly, the annoying rattle from my aerobars was a violation of Rule #65, and must be remedied.

If I was honest, breaking Rule #65 was a minor violation because I also violated Rule #54. This rule clearly orders, 'no aerobars on road bikes'. I felt a bit self-conscious with my clip-on aerobars because I was clearly flouting the rules. Not only that; aerobars were supposed to make me more aerodynamic and therefore faster. It was embarrassing when a peloton zoomed past as if I was standing still. However, I consoled myself by overtaking someone on a mountain bike. At least I preserved some of my road-cycling dignity.

As expected, midway through the ride my toes started hurting. The funny part was that they only hurt when I tried to wiggle them, checking if they were still attached to my feet. I suppose, moving the frozen digits would send some warm blood circulating, which brings the painful burning sensation. The wind and snow, and my frozen toes, made it seem like I was back in Winnipeg, except for cycling past animals at London Zoo. I had to stop and take a selfie with one of the giraffes who had also braved the elements, while its friends huddled inside. At least I wasn't the only one crazy enough to be out in that weather. Seeing that giraffe made me think that climbing Kilimanjaro would probably be similar. I smiled, and recalled Rule #9: 'if you are out riding in bad weather, it means you are a badass. Period'.

Sunday, 12 February 2017

Today's long run was tough. My legs were knackered from yesterday's bike ride, which was puzzling because I didn't push much. But I guess I haven't fully recovered from the distance that I covered on the bike yesterday morning. When I started the run, I was dejected by my slow pace. It felt like a brick session, which is beneficial for the triathlon. However, I'm not sure how it would affect my marathon training. I know I shouldn't worry too much about my marathon time, but it is still hard not to attempt to get close to my pace last year.

I was supposed to run for two hours and forty-five minutes today, and I calculated that if I did my normal route around Regent's Park, I would have to do three laps. I didn't want to do that, so last night I decided to take a different route and run to Hyde Park. The only problem was that I didn't know the exact route that would take me around two hours and forty-five minutes. I figured that, based on my pace last week, it would be about twenty-seven or twenty-eight kilometres. So the plan was to run for about thirteen or fourteen kilometres and then turn around and run back. This worked out well because as soon as I got to Hyde Park, I just kept on going to Buckingham Palace. It was cool running past the Royal Albert Hall, the Royal Artillery Memorial and Wellington Arch. It made me appreciate that I am incredibly privileged to be living in such a vibrant city full of wonderful places to explore. Buckingham Palace was already swarming with tourists very early on a Sunday morning, and I'm sure I photobombed a couple as I ran past them.

I used the Victoria Memorial as my turnaround point and as I started heading back, the arch of my left foot started hurting again. Alarmingly, the same thing happened during last week's long run. I struggled to figure out what could have caused it, with the uneven pavement the only thing coming to mind.

I varied my stride, but the pain wouldn't go away. I stopped a handful of times to readjust, and it eventually subsided, but it kept returning. With still more than ten kilometres to go, I was mentally drained and only had my last gel to help me get home. My spirit lifted after taking it and I made the slow, steady slog the mostly uphill way back. I eventually stumbled home, and was lucky that it only started raining just before I walked through the door. The effort took it out of me, though, and I knew I would be pretty useless for most of the day.

My heart sank when Tania told me we're going to IKEA. Most men would probably agree that walking around IKEA like a lab rat forced to find their way out of a maze is not how we want to spend a Sunday afternoon. I was yawning the whole way around, and just wanted to curl up on one of the sofas on display to rest my tired legs. I would have gladly done another five kilometres rather than be herded like cattle around the IKEA labyrinth. But I had no choice but to suck it up, because I had just spent almost three hours running and now I had to do my dad/husband duty. Granted, the things we bought didn't need assembly, so when we got home, I headed straight to the couch for a nap.

Last night, I watched a documentary called *Heart: Flatline to Finish Line*. It was about a group of triathletes who have heart problems and have had heart surgery. The film followed their emotional journey from their hospital beds, to attempting to finish an Ironman. It was inspirational, but right from the beginning, the main athlete says that he knows not everyone will finish the race. This brought home the enormity of the challenge that I will undertake. In the film, one person sadly didn't make the start line because he passed away, leaving behind his wife and a young son. I can't help but think about my mortality and the risks I am taking with this sport. I tried not to dwell on this too much, but I did make a note to get an appointment with my doctor and ask them to sign my form for the Paris Marathon.

The film also made me appreciate how much support I had been getting from Tania and the girls. I couldn't help but tell her how thankful I was for her encouragement and her putting up with my sporting endeavours. It is clear that most athletes wouldn't be capable of doing the Ironman without their family's help, and it's especially true for me.

'Enjoy the journey' – this quote from the film resonated with me a lot. It made me realise that the race itself is just a small part of the challenge. Getting to the starting line of any event is an achievement in itself, because all the training that has to be put in is rewarding on its own. I reflected about this when I was running this morning, and was grateful that I'm on this path. While appreciating this, it immediately released some endorphins, giving me that runner's high as I continue to enjoy my journey with a smile.

Tuesday, 14 February 2017

Yesterday was extremely busy; non-stop all day long. I got up early because I wanted to get to the pool and be back before 9am. Sofia is on half-term, so I have to look after her all week. And unless I can convince her to come for a run with me on her bike, I have to deal with an interrupted training week. I needed to be back before Tania had to start work, hence my early swim start yesterday. Juggling family life, work, social life and training is a challenge in itself. The key is to be flexible and modify your training schedule to suit whatever is happening during the week.

When I got to the pool, my legs were still tired from Sunday's hard run, so I knew that I needed to take it easy but I still wanted to swim at least 2.5 kilometres. As I started my warm-up laps, I was full of energy. But as soon as I got into the main set, it seemed like somebody turned off the switch. I experienced the same weariness like in previous races, where my legs and body were barely responding. At that point, I reasoned that it was effective training to prepare me mentally for the long Ironman swim. It was essential to visualise myself in a race, as it would lessen the chances of me panicking and should help me relax and continue on the day. So I eased my breathing, slowed down and pushed through to find a manageable pace. It was still tough, and I kept having to push away negative thoughts such as, *how will I ever finish swimming nearly four kilometres when I'm already exhausted, and not even halfway there? Not to mention cycle 190 kilometres and run a marathon afterwards!* These thoughts were hard to dismiss, but I found if I focused on my breathing or my stroke it helped to keep them at bay. I eventually clocked up 2.3 kilometres and cut the workout short. It was an effortful swim, but the mental preparation was valuable, so a useful session overall.

 I managed to get back home for 9am, where my day began. Elisa also had to stay home from nursery in the morning because one of her teachers was doing a home visit. If looking after a three-year-old while struggling to answer emails and sneak in some actual work doesn't sound busy, I don't know what does. The day was manic, as I also had an IKEA delivery to deal with, and then Elisa's teacher visited to explain about a new programme they're trialling to help kids start learning to read. After that, I had to call the IKEA courier because they had forgotten one item. Fortunately, they found it and returned sometime later. I then dropped off Elisa and her teacher at the nursery, and when I got back home, my next task was to assemble a chest of drawers, a new wardrobe and Elisa's new bed. I'd thought that it would only take me a few hours, but I was sorely mistaken. It didn't start well as I realised that the chest of drawers was too small. Tania and I had had a huge discussion about that and I was adamant about getting the smaller size, while she had wanted to get the bigger one. So I had to swallow my pride and admit that I was wrong and she was right. I know that admitting we're wrong is something that most men never do, but I don't have a problem with bruising my ego. Plus, I have a terrific wife who rarely says, "I told you so" and barely rubs my face in it. And to show how truly incredible she is, she even volunteered to drive back to IKEA and exchange the item, albeit begrudgingly.

What I thought would take two or three hours ended up taking bloody ages! I looked at my watch, and it was 11.05pm. I was exhausted, and I still had six drawers to assemble. I did a quick calculation and figured out what the cut-off time for the Ironman would be if we started at 6am and had seventeen hours to complete it. Again, it dawned on me just how long and tough the event would be. I realised that, if assembling this furniture were a long-distance triathlon, I would have failed to complete it within the time. (Although it's arguable that building IKEA furniture is tougher than doing an Ironman.) When I eventually finished at 12.30am, with an aching back, sore forearms and bloody hands, it did feel like completing a long-distance race. Elisa's smile this morning when she saw her new bed was priceless, and felt just as good as getting a finisher's medal. My own smile was as bright as hers.

Friday, 17 February 2017

The weather was warmer today, and I set off leisurely early without rushing. I was looking forward to a relaxed, easy run. However, it was anything but pleasurable. I was conscious of my stride, and paid attention to my left plantar fascia. I was making sure that the pain wouldn't come back, and probably overcompensated with my right leg, resulting in a tightness around my right quads. Then the dull pain returned, but it seemed to be a bit more to the side of my foot. I forgot to do the suggested remedy for plantar fasciitis that I read on the Internet, so I stopped, leaned on a tree and stretched my calves.

When I got going again it was better, but I found the whole run taxing. Perhaps I was overthinking it as opposed to just running and letting my natural stride take control. If I continue doing the stretches, it should eventually go away. Hopefully, by this Sunday when I do my long run. Thankfully, it's a recovery week this week, so the long run is relatively short at an hour-and-a-half.

While I was running, a thought popped into my head about the Buddhists' Four Noble Truths, so I looked them up afterwards. The first truth is that all life is suffering, pain and misery. The second is that this suffering is caused by selfish craving and personal desire. The third is that this craving can be overcome. The fourth is that the way to do so is through the Eightfold Path. Perhaps the first two truths can be applied to my current pursuits. It seems that, lately, my running has been all about suffering and pain. I certainly agree that this has been caused by my selfish craving and personal desire to complete the challenges that I've set myself. I'm glad to know that this craving can be overcome, although I'm not sure how that truth can be applied to my current situation. I certainly don't want to give up and not do my challenges. Perhaps the answer is via the fourth truth, and I will have to follow the Eightfold Path in my journey towards running enlightenment.

Apparently, in Japan, there are marathon monks who live around the mountains of Kyoto. In their quest for enlightenment, legend has it that they run a thousand marathons in a thousand days. Those who succeed become human Buddhas or living saints. I'm not saying that this is something that I will ever attempt, as it's rare for even a monk to attempt it. But I'll be happy enough to reach my own definition of running enlightenment: being able to run without any pain and suffering. I just hope that I don't have to run a thousand marathons in a thousand days in order to attain this nirvana.

Saturday, 18 February 2017

'Broken glasses, but not broken dreams'. That was the post that I put on my fundraising page for Cancer Research. A picture of me with my broken sunglasses accompanied it. I also added a picture of Elisa, expecting some sympathy and persuading people to donate. I'm doing pretty well, as I have raised £215 so far. Less than 80% away towards my goal of raising £1,000 for charity.

I had a pleasant training ride this morning, with the weather a balmy 7°C, which was way warmer than last week. I noticed that the rattling from my aerobars was gone, so the day was off to an excellent start.

I planned to do ten laps around Regent's Park for a total of about sixty kilometres. I warmed up by pedalling softly to the park. Once there, I settled into a rhythm and got into the tuck position on my aerobars as much as possible. The first couple of laps were okay, but by the third, my legs woke up and I pumped faster and produced more power. I wondered where this new-found form came from. I knew that I only have a ninety-minute run tomorrow, so I thought, *why not push it and see how my legs respond?* I was thrilled that I could put more power down and it was still comfortable. Then I was even more astonished when I started passing people; not just cyclists on their commute to work, or a hired 'Boris Bike', but actual roadies in proper Lycra. But then my confidence was dashed when a peloton zoomed past me. I realised that they were part of a cycling club, so I didn't mind too much. I'd thought that the goal was to get comfortable in an aero position and go at a steady pace. I had to remind myself that I'm training for a 190-kilometre ride, not a forty-kilometre time trial.

As I was entertaining these thoughts, another group of cyclists overtook me. They were from the same club, but I noticed that they were going at a slightly slower pace than the first group. I was able to stay at the rear of them and keep my pace, but when the road kicked up, the peloton started to slow down, so I decided to push harder to overtake. As I took the lead, I was committed and had to stay in front for as long as possible, or at least until we stopped at the lights. Nothing worse than being leapfrogged and having your ego handed to you on a plate. So I kept pushing, and noticed that two guys had stayed on my wheel and were drafting behind me. Again, I was bemused my legs were still solid and my breathing only increased by a fraction. So I flicked the gears to increase the pace some more to see what happened. As I cranked away, my legs kept getting stronger and stronger, and had to suppress a grin as I finally experienced a bit of what cyclists call 'form'. Yes, I was on form, and I loved it. It was that wonderful feeling where you're like flying and your legs are in harmony with your machine. My grin was now ear to ear, and by the time I looked back, I'd even lost the two guys who'd been slipstreaming behind me. *Wow! The training must be starting to pay off.* What a stark contrast from last week!

I kept the pace for most of the ride and then decided to ease off for the last two laps. I didn't want to completely shatter my legs because I still have to run tomorrow. The ride was brilliant, though, and when I got home, my perceived effort wasn't too bad. Psychologically, it will help build some confidence towards the Ironman. It took me just under two-and-a-half hours to do sixty kilometres. In theory, if I ride at the same pace for the Ironman, I should be capable of completing the cycle in about seven-and-a-half hours. What a fantastic way to start my weekend.

Sunday, 19 February 2017

At one-and-a-half hours, today's long run was shorter, but the training plan called for a half-marathon pace for the last thirty minutes. At first I thought my legs would be heavy after yesterday's ride, but they moved alright after the warm-up. The weather was warmer and I was rather hot, but I decided not to take off my toque (or beanie hat, as the English would call it). I thought that it would be useful to train while feeling hot because Paris will probably be warmer than London. Once I settled down, I decided to push the pace. Surprisingly, by running faster, my form improved. Perhaps it was psychological, but I felt lighter on my feet, and that the impact was not as hard compared to running at a slower pace. My heart rate was higher than normal, but for some reason, I was relaxed, and I could sustain the faster pace. Maybe the training is working, and I am getting fitter. So I just let my mind wander, without focusing on the physical effort.

A lot of things were going through my head today; among which was how I ended up living in the UK, since London was only supposed to be a one-month holiday!

After my first backpacking trip in Australia, I was bitten hard by the travel bug, and fortunate enough to subsequently go on other trips. I had a little holiday in Mexico, and then travelled to Thailand, two years after coming back from Oz. I never really settled in Winnipeg again after my travels, and I didn't seek a permanent job. Instead, I took the entrepreneur route and launched two tech start-up companies one after the other. I earned some money by editing technical books and co-authoring a book about computer programming. Funding for the two start-ups eventually ran out, as did the advance that I received for writing the book. Eventually, I took on a six-month software development contract to get me through. While I was doing the developer gig, I saw a cheap flight from Winnipeg to London advertised and thought that the timing would be perfect, as I could go as soon as my contract was up. A month-long trip around Europe would be cool, and I needed to scratch my travel itch. However, as soon as I booked my flights, the company I was contracted with decided to offer me a full-time position.

This was a difficult opportunity to pass up. On the one hand, I would have a steady job to come back to after my jaunt in Europe. On the other, a job offer seemed like a trap. I didn't think that I wanted to end up in Winnipeg. In the end, I decided to decline the offer because, in the back of my mind, I was seeking more of an adventure elsewhere.

So, in June 2003, I flew to London on what was supposed to be a one-month trip. I had return flights booked because that was part of the airline promotion; plus I had to get back to Winnipeg for my cousin's wedding, since I was one of the ushers. However, before leaving, I applied for a working holiday visa, just in case I decided to stay longer. Perhaps I always knew that I would try and stay to work in the UK. The booked return flight was just a safety net, in case things didn't work out. Later on, I got an email from my sister, telling me how sad my mom was after I left. I guess she knew before I did that I'd left home permanently. She was right, because I ended up missing my cousin's wedding and have lived in London ever since.

The one thing that terrified me before coming to London was that the big city would somehow chew me up and spit me out, and I would end up begging around the Tube stations. As I breathed hard during today's run, I was thankful for not ending up that way, and that I have built a wonderful life in this city. I smiled and thought that life is good, and then ran faster.

Saturday, 25 February 2017

Our third date hike. Tania and I were sticking to the plan and getting in at least one hike per month as part of our preparations for climbing Kilimanjaro. As parents, it's rare for us to spend time with just the two of us, so having the opportunity to spend most of the weekend without the kids was like being on holiday. We dropped them off at Tania's parents' early in the morning, then went to the Chiltern Hills. The Chilterns is considered as an Area of Outstanding Natural Beauty (AONB) in England, and I couldn't agree more with that description. We found a 17.5-kilometre route that I estimated would take us about four hours to complete. When we got on the trail, it was immediately apparent that it would be a challenging day. Not just in terms of distance, but also the hills that we had to negotiate. At one point, we were merrily chatting along down a tiny road with a very steep gradient and when we reached the bottom, Tania checked her GPS then looked at me with worry and said, "I think we took a wrong turn." I whined and said, "No!" I looked back up the road, which was like a wall from my vantage point. It was so skinny that it could barely fit a car, and it wasn't even one-way. I don't mind Tania navigating because there are no arguments when we get lost. So I shook my head, turned around and put one pole in front of the other. At least it wasn't my fault this time.

Apart from that one mistake, we managed to stay on piste the whole way around. We even encountered a creature with terrible tusks and terrible claws in Wendover Woods. At first, I was confused like a little mouse, then giddy when I realised it's the Gruffalo. We had to take a photo with him as we've read the book countless times with Sofia and Elisa. We couldn't wait to take the girls to see it. I had no idea that hiking could be so enjoyable, and a fantastic recreational activity. Tania and I are counting the years until Elisa is a bit older so that we can start to take both girls with us. Being outdoors is really gratifying, even if the weather is miserable, as long as you're wearing the right clothing. Like today, for example; it was overcast the whole day, and we had some rain. When we were climbing Coombe Hill, we were quite exposed to the wind, and at one point I thought I might be blown over. Luckily, I held upright; perhaps the deep mud kept me stuck to the ground. The weather wasn't perfect, but we still had a pleasurable time, and we learned that all of the gear that we're planning to take to Kilimanjaro is up to the task.

When we got back to London, we were exhausted, and decided to have a quick nap before going out to dinner. We wanted to make the most of not having the kids for the weekend. The problem was that, when we woke up, Tania's back was sore, which was a concern because her osteopath thought that she might need an MRI to see what's been causing her back pain. Plus, during the hike, Tania had felt something in her back but it wasn't painful enough for her to stop. The problem is that Kilimanjaro is not just a one-day hike. It is seven consecutive days of climbing, so if she's having problems now, we have to make sure we sort it out. She took some ibuprofen and that helped manage the pain, and we enjoyed a night out.

Sunday, 26 February 2017

My legs were stiff and fatigued this morning. However, since we didn't have the kids, we both had a delightful lie-in and for once I got to sleep past 7am!

The extra rest was helpful, because my training programme called for a half-marathon race today. I hadn't signed up for a race, but I'd wanted to simulate a race situation as much as possible, which meant trying not to stop. But that was before doing a four-hour hike yesterday. I wasn't sure if my legs would even move today, let alone run twenty-one kilometres, so I decided to do some light stretches, which I don't normally do. Then I followed my usual routine of eating breakfast and headed out the door. I figured that I should start running and see what happened.

The first two-and-a-half kilometres were a real struggle. I abandoned the idea of simulating a half-marathon race, and had to stop several times. My body was sluggish, and my legs were still asleep. I couldn't settle my breathing or relax at all. Then I noticed that it was a lot warmer, so I removed my gloves and hat and unzipped my jacket, then calmed my breathing and set off slowly once again. I hit a downhill section, and my legs could move again without seeming like there were lead weights attached to them. It's funny how my tiny adjustment could make such a difference. After that, I began to relax and picked up the pace. It was a complete change; like somebody had flicked a switch and turned on my whole body and brain. I started flying. I thought about continuing with a race simulation, but it wasn't possible because there were roads I had to cross, and therefore I had to wait for the green man. It wouldn't be smart to risk getting hit by a car just so I could simulate a half-marathon. Nevertheless, I was conscious of my pace, and I tried to run fast, but at a steady pace; similar to what I would need to run for a marathon. I focused on my posture and stride, and especially my breathing. When I stopped my watch and looked at my time, it said 1:59:41. Incredibly, I had gone under two hours (albeit by only nineteen seconds). If I doubled that for a full marathon distance, in theory, it meant I could run the marathon in under four hours. I knew that this would not be the case at all and that I probably needed a faster pace, but it was good enough for me today.

    I walked back home with a smile and planned the brilliant idea I had whilst running. My friend Slater will be the first of us to turn forty, and I'd thought of a perfect present for him. I want to create a collage of our travel photos and get it printed on a big canvas. I did this for Tania some years ago, and I love looking at it. Each photo evokes such fond memories and always brings a smile. I will do the same for Slater; I'm looking forward to creating it, and bringing a smile to his face too.

Tuesday, 28 February 2017

I wasn't sure what was on the marathon training plan when I woke up, so I was pleasantly surprised to see that I was supposed to have a day off from running. However, with the triathlon in mind, I decided to do an hour on the turbo trainer instead. Midway through the workout, I thought about my daily affirmations. A practice that I've been following for years, which I learnt from reading several books about successfully achieving your goals. I've learned the importance of writing down your goals and affirming them every day. The idea is that by visualising and repeating your goals daily, they will get imprinted in your subconscious. This should help motivate you, as well as attract opportunities that will lead to attaining them. So as I turned the pedals, I affirmed the following:

> *In an easy and relaxed manner; in a happy, healthy and positive way. In its own perfect time and for the highest good of all.*[3]

I followed this with a list of my intended goals. The first is 'to be successful together'. Like most people, I want to be successful. However, I figured out long ago that I have to define my own meaning for success. My success doesn't mean comparing myself to others, or struggling to live up to someone else's definition of being successful. To me, success is being happy and fulfilled in all aspects of my life. It means being successful in my family life, my social life; being healthy, personally fulfilled and financially stable. As well as to give back in some way. Those are my criteria for success, and I strive to strike a balance in achieving it all equally. This balance is important because to me being successful in just one part of your life is not ideal. For example, I've seen people work so hard to make a lot of money and achieve financial success, but in doing so, they sacrifice their family and/or health. What is the point of having all that money, at the cost of losing your family and/or not being

---

[3] This is a slightly modified version of one of Marc Allen's affirmations: https://marcallen.com

healthy enough to enjoy it? By the same token, I don't want to be successful all by myself. I would like to achieve success along with Tania; for her to achieve her definition of success, and for us to be successful together. I figure there is no point in getting to the top and finding I'm all by myself up there. I would rather be there with someone else, as well as having many of my friends with me so that we can have one massive party!

I find my daily affirmations meditative and spiritual in some way. This practice is a powerful tool that helps guide me. They put me in the right frame of mind, and start my day positively. I finish my daily affirmations with the following mantra:

Support, encourage, grow and love each other along the journey.
Constant and never-ending improvement.
Life is good.
Thank you, thank you, thank you.

Wednesday, 01 March 2017

I can't believe we're into March! Just over a month to go until the Paris Marathon. Training is going well, and it seems that I'm getting faster. I did an interval run today, with ten-minute intervals followed by a two-minute recovery, repeated three times. My overall pace was 5:36/km, which is around the marathon pace that I need to run. During the run, I thought about how running a marathon used to be an impossibility for me, and the long journey I took to make that impossibility a reality.

Growing up in the Philippines, I was not into sports at all. I was a chubby kid who spent a lot of time watching TV and playing with Lego. I did ride my bike around the neighbourhood with my friends, but only on weekends, and that was the extent of my outdoor activity. I never learned how to swim because there were no pools where we lived.

My family moved to Canada the summer before my thirteenth birthday. When we got there, my cousin pointed out that I was pretty overweight and should watch what I ate. Those comments made me rather conscious of my diet. In the Philippines, we had typically eaten rice three times a day, whereas in Canada this was cut down to just dinner time, and only five or six times a week. By cutting down my carbohydrate intake, I started to lose some of my baby fat. I wouldn't say I started to get lean, but at least I wasn't noticeably overweight during my early teens.

By the time I reached sixteen, I was your typical Canadian teenager, and I started thinking about bulking up so that I could impress the girls. My friends and I joined a gym, and we started lifting weights. I gained some muscle, and my overall physique did look better, but sadly it didn't help me at all with impressing girls. I continued lifting weights throughout my high-school years and up until I started university. At university the amount of time I spent in the gym decreased drastically – because of the studying required, but mostly because I was legally allowed to drink alcohol, and so I did a lot more partying rather than hitting the weights.

At uni, I started to do more cardio instead of just lifting weights. The university gym had an indoor track in the basement which was known as 'the Gritty Grotto'. It was dusty, dank and dark, with dirt on all sides, exposed pipes and ducts, and a low ceiling you could easily reach. It would get musty down there, and almost always smelled like sweaty socks. But during the long, harsh Winnipeg winters, there was nowhere else to run, really, so that was where everybody ran. I took up running at the Gritty Grotto to build my cardio fitness, but mainly because that was where all the fit girls were. I probably did get fitter – or, more realistically, barely maintain my fitness level – but sadly I don't recall ever meeting a girl at the Grotto. I do remember struggling to keep up and run behind some, but I always got really bad shin splints, and I could never do more than twenty minutes around the track.

One day in class, my friend Kyle mentioned that his dad had run a marathon when he was younger. That blew me away; I was awestruck. I couldn't comprehend how I could ever go from barely fit enough to run twenty minutes without a lot of pain, to running a full marathon. It was an unachievable goal. I was astonished to find out that Kyle's dad had done it. Perhaps that was the first time the idea of running a marathon entered my head, even though at the time it wasn't even remotely possible for me. It was nearly ten years before I completed my first marathon in Amsterdam in 2008. A lot had happened in that time, but I managed to turn something I thought was impossible into reality.

I thought of that while I was running today. Now, I'm on a similar journey to attempt my first Ironman. Ten years ago, finishing a triathlon, let alone an Ironman, was a complete impossibility because I couldn't even swim a length of a pool. Even a couple of years ago, I didn't think I was ready to tackle a full Ironman, even though I had completed a number of Olympic-distance and half-Ironman races. It is funny looking back and thinking how far I've come. As I considered this, I said my mantra: "Life is good. Thank you, thank you, thank you!" I finished the run with a smile.

Thursday, 02 March 2017

Returning to Winnipeg following my travels in Australia back in 2000, I had a whole new outlook on life. I was brimming with confidence, and optimistic that I could do anything. One of the things I'd learned during my travels was a quote that went: 'Experience is what you get when you don't get what you want'. This message stuck with me, and I realised that there is no reason not to try and do something because even if I don't succeed, I'm still much better for trying it as I gain experience from the attempt. After this powerful realisation, I wasn't afraid of failing in attempting something new. So when my friend Bruce asked me to join his company's marathon relay team in the summer of 2001, I said yes immediately.

That relay was the first race I ever did. Bruce's company had put together a team to run the 2001 Manitoba Marathon, but they were short one guy, so I volunteered to join them. I didn't do much training, so I was assigned the shortest leg, which was around 7.88 kilometres. The whole race atmosphere was exciting, and I went in with a strategy of chasing down pretty girls. I'd look for a hot girl who was ahead of me, then run hard to catch up to her, then check her out while trying to pass her, looking cool and nonchalant while doing so. Then I'd look for the next girl further up the road and repeat the process. Back then I didn't think about pacing or anything; I just wanted to run down as many girls as I could. I guess it was some form of interval running. I remember almost missing the relay exchange point because I couldn't quite get past the last girl I was chasing. Luckily Bruce saw me run past him and screamed my name so that I could hand off to the next guy. I enjoyed that race, and the following year I planned to run a half-marathon. Which I did, and I continued to do so annually until I ran my first full marathon in 2008 in Amsterdam. That same year, I did my first triathlon, and since then instead of running a half-marathon every year, I've been doing triathlons.

It was amusing thinking about that first race while I was doing my easy run today. Well, 'easy' is a relative term because I attempted to run slow but for some reason it felt laboured. Perhaps because it was windy this morning; so strong it blew me sideways, plus there were times when I almost tripped because the wind blew my raised leg into my other leg. I'm glad it was only a short run since the weather conditions were miserable.

Yesterday I went to my local GP to get my medical certificate signed for the Paris Marathon. One of the requirements for the race is to get my doctor to sign me off as having no complications barring me from participating in running competitions. The only problem was that my GP wouldn't sign it because the form says that I should have a medical exam done. Since the NHS doesn't cover medical examinations for athletic events, they would need to charge me £120. I thought this was a bit excessive considering that the cost of the race itself was less. The receptionist said that an alternative was for my GP to write me a letter saying that he doesn't see any reason why I can't run based on my medical records. However, I suspect their records for me are limited because I've consulted the NHS only three times in the whole time I've been living in the UK.

In the past thirteen-and-a-half years, I've been to a hospital twice. Once was when I fell off a five-metre wall while I was bouldering at a climbing gym. I dislocated my left elbow, which I managed to pop back in myself, but went to A&E anyway to have it checked out. The second time was after I did a mile-long open-water swim in the River Thames. My eye became severely irritated, and I had to see an eye doctor. I thought it was probably due to the river water, but apparently it was because my eyelashes were wet and the lashes had somehow got into my eye and scratched it when I blinked. The only time I had visited my local GP for myself was a couple of months ago, to ask for a referral to get the old 'snip' done. Tania and I are happy with the two girls we have, and we don't want any accidents, so we figured getting a vasectomy is the way to go. However, because the NHS is at breaking point, I'm still on the waiting list. I was expecting that they would do it at the beginning of the year, but now I wish they'd schedule it for just after the marathon. Anyway, I digress – the main point is that I don't think my GP will have enough information on my health based on that one visit, so I'm not sure what they'll put in the letter.

When I got home, I did some quick Internet research and found out what other people have done. It seems a lot of people are in the same boat, and it all depends on the individual GP as to whether they sign the form or not. (It has something to do with whether their practice insurance would cover it.) One person suggested that I should take up smoking, drink loads of alcohol and gain loads of weight – if I were sick, the doctor would give me a free medical exam on the NHS. I considered it, but thought it might be counterproductive. The general advice is to forge a signature on the form. Apparently, the medical form is required for all races in France to cover the organiser's insurance. Although the forgery is straightforward enough, it is illegal, so I plan to pay for a letter from my GP and get them to sign the form when I pick it up.

Saturday, 04 March 2017

I decided to do my long run today (thirty kilometres) instead of tomorrow because Tania is going out tonight for a friend's hen party (she is the maid of honour). I've learned my lesson, and know that I won't get a decent night's sleep because I'll probably stay up waiting for her. Therefore, I figured I should switch my Saturday and Sunday workout plans. So tomorrow, depending on how much sleep I get and how tired I am, I'll do an easy bike ride. However, after today's run, my quads were shot, and it was hard going up and down the stairs. I'll be shocked if I can turn the pedals tomorrow.

I wasn't sure I could do my normal route today because part of the road to Regent's Park was closed yesterday due to an unexploded World War II bomb in Brondesbury Park. We live relatively close to where they discovered the bomb, but we weren't evacuated. I always say that London is a vibrant, dynamic city to live in, but this is just a little close to home. Luckily, when

I got to Brondesbury Park, the road was clear, and it seemed that the army had successfully disposed of the bomb.

This week I've added planks as part of my core body workout that I do after each run, and it made a difference to my overall pace. I've noticed that in the later stages of a run when I am getting tired, my posture will start to suffer – I probably bend at the waist more as opposed to holding my body straight. Strengthening my core will help me maintain my running posture for longer, and in effect hold my stride in the latter stages. But doing the plank is agony. I don't know why, but somehow this exercise breaks Einstein's theory of relativity because I swear time slows right down when I'm in the position. A minute seems to last an eternity, and then the same minute during recovery in-between reps seems to go faster than the speed of light. It's perplexing to me how one exercise can defy the laws of physics.

I finished my long run today at my local park, and was happy to see some Parkrun friends. They had just finished doing the weekly Parkrun and were chilling out at the cafe. I said hello and explained to them why I haven't been doing Parkrun lately, due to the conflict with my marathon and triathlon training. I did say that after the Paris Marathon I should be able to volunteer for one or two weekends while I recover. I do miss Parkrun, especially because it doesn't take up three hours of my Saturday morning!

After the immediate glow of the run, and once I'd finished my stretches, the inevitable exhaustion hit me. It was a struggle because I have to look after the girls by myself all day, so it was a mission to get through the rest of the day. Sofia decided that they wanted to make some cupcakes, so this kept them busy for a bit, while I rested my legs and nodded off on the sofa. It was enough to give me some energy to take them swimming. I figured it would be a productive way to spend the afternoon; plus it would tire them out so that they'd go to bed early tonight.

The pool was wonderful, but I could barely move my legs, so I made up a new game to see who could lie down and float for the longest. I managed to beat both girls every time. We enjoyed the pool, but what wasn't cool was at the end when Elisa was complaining that her tummy hurt. I was sure that it was just gas, and so I urged her to burp or fart to let it out. She farted in the showers, which gave her some relief, but as we were getting changed, she was still in pain. So I told her to try and burp, which in hindsight was a mistake because instead she ended up puking up her lunch. It was pretty gross to see all the chunks of grapes and frankfurters, but I caught all of her vomit in my towel, so the clean-up job wasn't so bad. My plan worked, because they were both exhausted, so I got some time to relax for most of the evening.

Tuesday, 07 March 2017

It was supposed to be an easy run today, but much as I tried, it wasn't at all easy. My right quads were bugging me, and it seems I was overworking it. Perhaps my quads hadn't fully recovered from last Saturday's long run. It appeared that in running slowly, my form suffered. I probably overcompensated and put more pressure on my quads when I landed, as opposed to leaning forward more to ease the impact on my legs. Or maybe I was overanalysing it.

At some point during the run, I started thinking about something else. Earlier this morning I saw a friend of mine at Elisa's nursery. A few local dads had arranged to see a movie tonight, but he couldn't make it because he had to go to a friend's fortieth birthday celebrations. It got me thinking about my upcoming fortieth birthday, and whether or not all these challenges constituted a midlife crisis.

> *The term midlife crisis was first coined in 1965 where early analysis suggested that it could happen anywhere between the ages of 40 and 60, but it is now shown to start much earlier.*[4]

I researched a lot of sites on the Internet listing all sorts of signs of a male midlife crisis, and I believe all of them. After reading these sites, it seems that all males are in a constant midlife crisis, and have been since puberty. Taking *The Telegraph*'s 'Top 40 signs of having a midlife crisis' as an example, it was hard to find anyone I know who is *not* having a crisis. Number 2 on their list is 'still going to music festivals like Glastonbury'. Also, 'obsessively comparing your appearance with others the same age' – doesn't everybody do that? I particularly like Number 35: 'hangovers get worse and last more than a day on occasions'. But some things on the list do strike home, such as Number 8 ('splashing out on an expensive bike'), Number 21 ('start dyeing your hair when it goes grey') and Number 38 ('take up triathlons or another extreme sport')! I guess if I go by these criteria, I must be in a full-blown midlife crisis. Granted, I'd only dyed my hair once, and technically I bought my expensive bike two years ago, so maybe that doesn't count. Plus, I had been doing triathlons for nine years, so I hadn't just taken up the sport. The most telling sign that I was probably *not* experiencing a midlife crisis was that I was not suffering from anxiety or depression, which, according to the NHS website, are two of the main symptoms. The NHS says that 'a midlife crisis can happen when men think they've reached life's halfway stage and feel time is running out'. Well, I certainly don't think that time is running out. However, I think I'm about to reach a significant milestone, and perhaps this had been the catalyst for me to attempt these challenges. I

---

4 'Top 40 signs of a midlife crisis revealed' by Radhika Sanghani: http://www.telegraph.co.uk/news/newstopics/howaboutthat/10156725/Top-40-signs-of-a-midlife-crisis-revealed.html

suppose for some people turning forty could be depressing, but personally, I would use it more positively to make an effort and accomplish things that I want to do.

I think I'm fine for now and there is no midlife crisis as such. What worries me more is further down the road: 'some men develop depression, loss of sex drive, erectile dysfunction, and other physical and emotional symptoms when they reach their late 40s to early 50s. Read more about the so-called male menopause'.[5] Yikes; I'm glad that is still a number of years down the line. Compared to the male menopause, the midlife crisis sounds like a walk in the park.

Wednesday, 08 March 2017

What a wet and windy Wednesday. The rain soaked me to the bone during my interval run. I did find it enjoyable in some way, and I wasn't completely miserable. I savoured being tough and hard running in the rain, and I thought about the first time I entered an adventure race in Winnipeg.

On my way home from my gap year after university, I did another two weeks in New Zealand to explore the South Island. When we planned our Australia trip, the idea was to go for three months. Two weeks in Fiji, followed by two weeks in New Zealand and the remainder in Australia. That time in New Zealand was epic, and we travelled through the North Island on the Kiwi Experience bus tour, also known as the 'big green party machine'. The bus travelled from city to city, stopping at famous sites and then having a huge binger wherever we ended up for the night. Plus, we did some crazy extreme sports like bungee jumping, white-water rafting and skydiving along the way. It was an exciting way to travel and meet remarkable people

---

5 NHS website. The 'male menopause': https://www.nhs.uk/conditions/male-menopause/

from around the world, while we partied together around New Zealand. However, since we only planned on staying two weeks in New Zealand, we only got as far as Picton on South Island before turning back. I was sad that I didn't get a chance to see most of the island, and that I had to say goodbye to our Kiwi Experience friends. So, on my way home after spending nearly six months in Australia, I went back to explore the rest of South Island. It turned out to be fairly easy to keep changing my return flight to Canada, so what was supposed to be a three-month trip ended up closer to seven months. Of all my friends, I was the penultimate person to go back to Winnipeg. The other guys stuck to the original schedule and headed back months before me.

By the time I got to South Island, I was travelling by myself, and I jumped on board another Kiwi Experience bus to explore the island on my own. Well, not really on my own because it was so easy to make friends on the bus, and after the first night of drinking, we were all one happy family partying our way through Kiwi Land.

One of the adventure stops on the tour was an opportunity to do a glacier hike on the Franz Josef Glacier. After the bungee jump, white-water rafting and skydiving, I needed to continue to fulfil my university dream of being 'Extreme Howie'. I had always liked watching extreme sports, and I fantasised doing 'extreme' adventures myself. The glacier hike sounded like an adrenaline rush, and I was eager to go, so I didn't hesitate to sign up.

For the hike, we were split into groups according to our ability, and I was put in the middle group. At the time, I was so caught up in the party atmosphere that I didn't think much about the actual physical challenge of hiking a glacier. Within about twenty minutes of climbing, I was panting and breathing hard. I was out of my depth and there was no way for me to keep up with my group. So I stayed back and went up with the slowest group. I was sure that this was mostly due to the constant partying and drinking of the previous weeks, rather than me being completely unfit. (Or, more precisely, me being unfit due to the excess alcohol that I'd been shoving down my throat day in, day out.) So while trying to catch my breath on that glacier, surrounded by the most bluish ice I've seen, I made a conscious vow to myself to be fit all year long. That was a pivotal moment in my life.

I learned so many important lessons during my first travel experience, especially about myself and what I was capable of. I took them on board and strived to prove to myself that I can do anything I set my mind to. To follow through with my vow, I looked for races to enter when I got back to Canada. I found the Eco Adventure race in Winnipeg and signed up.

The Eco Adventure in Fort Whyte, Winnipeg, was an adventure race based on the Eco-Challenge expedition race that aired on the Discovery Channel from 1995 to 2002. The Eco-Challenge was a multi-day expedition race in which teams raced twenty-four hours a day over a rugged five-hundred-kilometre course, whereas the Eco Adventure was minuscule in comparison. But still, it was challenging for me. The first Eco Adventure race consisted of kayaking followed by a run with orienteering, then some rollerblading, and a final mountain-bike leg. I signed up two weeks before the race without any kayaking experience and barely able to rollerblade. Needless to say, I did barely any training for the event. The night before, I had to go to the local pool to get basic instructions on how to paddle in a kayak and learn what to do in case I tipped over!

Fortunately – or unfortunately, depending on how you look at it – the lake was still frozen on the day of the race. So, instead of kayaking *in* the lake, we had to carry our kayaks *around* the lake. That was back-breaking work, and the kayak I'd hired was probably the heaviest one. That race was tough, and it was my first lesson in being ill-prepared for a race. I didn't know anything about race nutrition, and had to ask my sister – who was part of my support crew – to run to the shop and buy me a chocolate bar because I was about to hit the wall. It was also the first time that I experienced cramps during a race. A severe cramp seized my calf muscles and I nearly fell over during the mountain-bike leg. Luckily, it was close to the end, and I managed to shake it out and eventually finish.

That was the first time I felt total elation upon finishing a race, and it was a feeling like no other. Perhaps I've been seeking to chase that sensation ever since. But sometimes I don't need to enter a race to experience that emotion; all I have to do is think about the memory, and I get to relive it all over again. During today's run, for example. As I finished the last few metres, I imagined myself crossing that finish line. The smile on my face was just as bright as when I finished the Eco Adventure.

Sunday, 12 March 2017

When I woke up today, my head hurt, and my mouth was parched, a clear sign of dehydration. My body was sore, I was exhausted and slightly dizzy. I stared at the ceiling trying to remember what happened last night.

I recalled doing my longest training run so far, and it was tough. It started off normally enough, and I got into a steady rhythm. The plan was to run thirty-two kilometres, so I set out to run to Regent's Park and then do four laps around it. For nutrition, I brought along four gels, planning to take one every forty minutes. (For the actual marathon, I plan to take seven or eight, and take a gel every twenty-five minutes.) Towards the end of the third lap, my pace started to drop, and I was fatigued. Then, when I turned around to start my fourth lap, another runner ran past me doing about 5:30/km. I could keep up with him, so I decided to run alongside and use him to pace myself.

In retrospect, this was where I made a mistake. I matched his pace the whole way around the park, even after he increased it to 5:25/km, which is faster than my intended marathon pace. I knew I was going too fast but stayed with him anyway because I thought I was getting my second wind. I held the pace until we finished the lap, at which point I had to stop for the traffic lights so that I could start running back home. As soon as I stopped, I realised that I might have pushed too hard. My legs started to seize up, and I couldn't focus. A clear sign of the early stages of 'bonking'. This is a phrase that athletes use when they hit the wall. Physically, it means a complete glycogen depletion. In other words, my body had run out of fuel.

It was a struggle to get going again, and every step was agony. I had one more gel left, but I wasn't due to take it for another twenty minutes. I said sod it, and gulped the sweet nectar. I needed it to get me home, which was still about six kilometres away. It got me moving, but I had to stop and walk a lot of the way home. It was awful, and I couldn't concentrate. I kept thinking of stopping and sitting down, and calling Tania to pick me up. At one point, it seemed like my brain was completely out of it and was wandering around 'la-la land' for a while, perhaps slightly hallucinating. I don't know how I managed it, but eventually I walked through the front door and collapsed in the hallway.

I did take away some lessons from the run. Number one is to always go at my own pace. In hindsight, it was silly of me to match the other runner. Number two is to always think about race nutrition. If I had taken more gels, I'm sure I would've been fine. Finally, it is a bad idea to eat KFC the night before a long run!

I was hesitant about eating it. It would probably have been better if I'd made some pasta so that I would have some carbs for the run. But I succumbed to the temptation and ate loads of chicken instead. I didn't eat much of anything else, and there were probably barely any carbohydrates in what I ate. Therefore,

I'm sure that contributed to me bonking. Learning all these lessons during training is important. Hopefully, I won't make the same mistakes on race day.

I switched my long run today to yesterday because I had a stag party to go to last night. It was my longest training run before the marathon and I didn't want to miss it. But after the disastrous bonking, I knew that there would be no way for me to make the first part of the stag party. The plan was to play golf in the afternoon, followed by a pub crawl in the evening. But I needed more time to recover, so I skipped the trip to the driving range and had a nap instead. After a couple of hours of shut-eye, I was well enough to eat something. Regrettably, I ate the leftover chicken, which wasn't too healthy. But I reckoned I'd burned enough calories for the day, so it was fine.

I eventually caught up with the stag party at the first scheduled pub. I didn't intend to drink too much because I was still tired from the run. However, the first pint of lager went down rather well – probably due to my dehydration – and I instantly got a buzz from the booze. By the time I had my second pint, and a shot of coffee tequila with the groom-to-be, all thoughts of training went out the window, and I was in full party mood. I can't remember how much I drank, but, judging from my hangover today, it was a significant amount.

I remember being a wingman for one of the guys, who, ironically, got divorced just two weeks ago. We approached four young ladies, and two of them turned out to be single. I was such an enthusiastic wingman that I even offered my services to one of the girls. It was amusing, and I managed to introduce her to some other random guy. It was easy for me to approach a group of women because, apparently, I look friendly and non-threatening. Plus, I don't have any intention of actually hitting on them, so I have no fears of rejection whatsoever. Once, at university, my friend's sister took me to the women's toilet of the bar so that we could smoke a spliff with her friends. She introduced me to all the girls who walked in as 'Howie, the non-threatening male'. The girls would then calm down after being shocked to find a man in their sanctuary.

The rest of the night was a blur, and I remember leaving the other guys at some club that had naked girls. It made me uncomfortable, so I said my goodbyes and grabbed a cab home. Overall, it was good times. It reminds me of my stag party, which was a three-day affair…

Tania and I got married in Ravello, which is on the Amalfi Coast of Italy. It was a wonderful wedding, and I loved every moment of it. Since most of my friends would be flying in from Canada or the USA, we decided to have my bachelor party in Rome the weekend before the wedding. There were six of us, all flying in from different cities, and we all met up in a hostel close to Rome's Termini Station. We felt like jet-setters, meeting up in such a fashionable city. I can't recall the whole evening, but I do remember having a Sharpie marker with us, and the guys went around asking girls to write something on my shirt or body. That was when I came up with the phrase 'Chase That Smile'. I wrote it on my friends' arms and explained to them what it meant to me. 'Chase That Smile' expressed what it was like to have found Tania and to be marrying her. It is like that feeling I get after finishing a race or accomplishing something significant; those bursts of euphoric joy and happiness after a good run, or the sudden explosion of endorphins that flood my brain while I'm training. It also refers to our constant journey together to find happiness, revel in it and bring a smile to all the people around us. I'm fortunate enough to experience all of this just from being with my wife. That night, I told my friends to continue chasing their smiles, and wished that they caught them every day.

That first night in Rome, we shut down every bar we went to, all the way back to the hostel. It was the early hours of the morning until we managed to get some sleep. Then the guys shook me awake and told me to pack my bags. I didn't know what they had planned, so I just did what I was told and jumped in the shower. While I was brushing my teeth in the communal sinks, wrapped only in my towel, a girl looked over and said, "Must've been a great night." I didn't know what she was referring to until I looked in the mirror and saw that all the Sharpie messages from the night before were still on my body. I beamed at her, and I just nodded in response.

Once we were ready, we jumped on the train, and the boys took me back to the airport. I'd had no idea they'd be kidnapping me and taking me somewhere else. It was the perfect surprise for me because, after we'd got back from Australia, every time we were out drinking, I would always say that I wanted to go to the airport and fly off somewhere. So in a way, the boys made my dream come true by whisking me off to Amsterdam to continue my bachelor party. I was impressed that they managed to pull it off. They were amazing, but it didn't end there. As if flying me to another country wasn't special enough, the guys did one better. After checking in at the hostel, Burton asked me to lead the way to the room. As I walked in, somebody jumped from the bunk bed and yelled 'surprise!' It took me a few seconds to recognise Kyle and so I was in complete shock. He couldn't come to the wedding and I wasn't expecting him to show up. He'd just started a teaching job at a college, and he couldn't take time off. So it was a total surprise to see him standing in our hostel room, and it took a long time to comprehend what was going on. I was pretty sure we hadn't smoked any weed yet, so it wasn't my imagination. It turned out that Kyle had flown to Amsterdam just for the weekend to celebrate my bachelor party and reunite Voltron. Even though he couldn't come to the wedding, him being at my bachelor party was the second-best thing. I can't appreciate enough how lucky I am to have such great friends.

Thursday, 16 March 2017

With my weakened immune system from the weekend long run and shenanigans, I've caught a bug from Elisa and have been unwell the last few days. But I had a restful night and feel much better today. I read my training plan and I'm supposed to do twenty-five minutes easy, followed by twenty minutes marathon pace and then another twenty-five minutes easy. When I went out, the first twenty-five felt harder than usual, even though I was trying to run as easy as I could. Perhaps I was still not well, but when I picked up the pace, I started feeling better. But mentally, the run was challenging. I was constantly fighting the urge to stop, even after my body adjusted to the pace. My brain was probably fighting the fact that I would need to run more than ten kilometres today, which is longer than my usual weekday run. I had to use all my mind tricks to get myself around. These included breaking down the run into manageable chunks, so, instead of thinking, *I have to run for over an hour today*, I told myself that I just needed to focus on the next five minutes. Then I worked out how far five minutes of running would get me at my current pace, and saw how close I could get with my guess. My other useful trick was diverting my attention to every stride. I focused on each body part, starting from my feet, then my ankles, and worked my way up to my knees, hips, abs, arms, shoulders, neck and head. I would spend some time on each area, making sure that I was aligned properly and moving correctly. This would help focus my mind and not dwell on any negative thoughts.

When I speak to people about running, some would say that they find it boring. My response is always the opposite. Most of the time I find running enjoyable and relaxing; even similar to meditation. It allows me to free my mind and let my thoughts wander. Today, towards the end of my run, I pictured myself finishing the Paris Marathon. I visualised the last twenty-five minutes of the race and what they would be like. I imagined myself being in the moment, running strong with determination, relishing the cheers of the crowd and encouraging all my fellow runners towards the line. I imagined the anticipation upon seeing the finish line, and holding my composure to ensure I didn't go for a crazy sprint at the end. Then I pictured crossing the line and releasing all my emotions from the past four hours of running. All the hard work from all the weeks and months of training, to chase that smile and catch it at the finish.

The visualisation was so powerful that, when I finished the run today, it was like I had already run Paris. Reminiscing old memories or imagining future events and experiencing them as if they are happening is why I enjoy running so much. I can easily immerse myself in certain experiences just by thinking about them. Plus, every time I complete a run, it's like I'm crossing an imaginary finish line, and I get a glorious sense of accomplishment. It never fails to bring a smile to my face.

Saturday, 18 March 2017

I'm 25% towards my fundraising goal! It's not going as quickly as I would like, but I'm grateful that people are supporting me. I've been posting weekly updates on my page, eagerly reminding my friends of what I'm doing and encouraging them to make a donation. I have an idea of having a barbecue at our house in the summer as a fundraising event. We can invite our friends and they can make a donation as an entry fee or something. Then we can put together a mini 'Scootathlon' for the kids. This is something Sofia did once; they ride their scooters for three hundred metres or so, then jump on their bikes for the same distance, and finally run at the end. It was good fun, and hopefully Tania and I can find the time to organise it.

Today I rode for seventy kilometres. I wanted to do seventy-five, but I miscounted the number of laps around Regent's Park and came up short. It was wet and gusty, which made it tough. I stayed down on my aerobars for most of it, which helped. Despite the poor weather, it was lovely to see the beautiful cherry trees blossoming. With the warmer temperature, it seems like spring is finally here. I saw some zebras and giraffes at London Zoo, and I imagined being on an African safari exploring the wild plains of Tanzania – which brought to mind that Tania and I still have a lot of things to purchase for our Kilimanjaro climb. That has taken a back seat in the past few weeks because of our garage renovation project. We've been so focused on designing and ordering all the things we need that we haven't had time to think about the trek. We need the builders to finish the garage soon, so that we can concentrate on Kilimanjaro again. And I hope that we'll have some money left to buy the other kit we still need.

Last night, I watched a film called *100 Metros*. It is about a guy who was diagnosed with multiple sclerosis (MS) and went on to complete an Ironman. The film was in Spanish with English subtitles. I was quite touched by it because I could easily relate to the main character. Ramón was thirty-five when he was diagnosed. At the time, he had one son and a pregnant wife. He set himself the challenge of completing an Ironman as a way to fight the disease. With the help of his father-in-law – who himself was grieving after losing his wife – he managed to complete the course on his second attempt. I was surprised to find out that the film was inspired by the true story of a man named Ramón Arroyo. It was such an inspiring film, and it made me contemplate several things. For one, I considered what I would do if I were faced with a similar condition. I didn't know much about MS, but apparently it can cause impaired movement (to the point where the person can't walk on their own), loss of the sense of touch and even blindness. It was gut-wrenching to watch the character not being able to hold his newborn son, and his fear of never seeing his children's faces one day. But he managed to overcome his struggles and eventually finish an Ironman. It just goes to show the power of sport, which can give a person hope and courage to overcome their adversities, whatever they might be. Every time I start a race, I look around and feel huge admiration for all the people racing with me. We've committed and sacrificed a lot just to get to that starting line, and each of us has gone through our personal journey to reach that point. There is a strong sense of camaraderie in knowing that, for the next few hours, we'll all be trying to conquer our own challenges in pursuit of our goals.

Monday, 20 March 2017

Yesterday was a tough day of running. I woke up not quite right; perhaps it was due to the previous day's bike ride. So I forced myself out the door and started the run. I thought it was weird that I felt dismal, especially because I'd managed to relax for most of Saturday. Well, after I took Elisa swimming, which was part of my dad duties for the day, so I didn't feel too guilty about relaxing on the couch afterwards. Chilling out on the sofa is always a fine line. If I've been productive, then it's well deserved; however, if I haven't done anything, I just feel lazy for sitting around. But on Saturday, the sofa was well earned. However, it should've given me a clue that all was not well.

Sofia had been sick with a fever since Friday, and I was not too sympathetic because I thought she was just playing up. Thankfully, by Sunday her fever had gone, but after I came back from my run, I knew that I wasn't well. By late afternoon, I was shivering and had a temperature of nearly 40°C. It served me right for not believing my daughter, and I did apologise to her for not caring enough when she was ill. I must've caught whatever she had, probably due to my immune system being weak from all the training. I still feel sick today, and I've decided to take the next couple of days off from training.

My long run yesterday didn't go well either. I planned to do two laps around Regent's Park; around twenty-five kilometres in total. However, after one lap, I turned back and headed home. I was taking it easy when, about four kilometres from home, I felt something in my left heel, so I stopped immediately. I massaged my Achilles tendon and walked for a bit, and then attempted to run again. After a couple of hundred metres, the pain came back, so I walked the rest of the way home. My head hung low, dejected, and thoughts of being hit with an injury were swirling around my mind. I did the right thing by stopping right away and not running any further. I pray that it's nothing and a couple of days off will sort it.

What got me through part of the run was thinking about how I proposed to Tania. Before she got pregnant with Sofia, we had planned to take a year off and go backpacking. It was 2007, and one of my goals was to travel around South America before I turned thirty. But due to the surprise pregnancy, we had to revise our plans and change it to a five-week trip. I quit my job with an investment bank and was looking forward to life on the road. A month before the trip, we had to go to Canada for my friend Roz's wedding, and also for my sister's wedding. While there, I bought Tania's engagement ring. I had thought that I would propose to her in Machu Picchu, but since we had to cut our travel plans short we were no longer going to Peru. We had decided to just visit Venezuela, Argentina and Brazil. When we left for Caracas, I didn't know how I would propose, but I figured an opportunity would present itself while we were on the road.

We arrived in Venezuela in September 2007, a day before my birthday, just in time to fulfil my goal of visiting South America before my thirtieth. It wasn't long before the right opportunity came about. The day after we celebrated my birthday, we took a day trip to an island. But when we stepped on shore, we saw litter strewn on the main beach. Disappointed, we continued walking around the island hoping to find a better spot. After leaving the main tourist area, we found a secluded beach that was pristine, clean and with no one else on it. We sat down and started enjoying the hot sun, and the turquoise – postcard-perfect – Caribbean Sea. With no one in sight, I gave Tania a sly look and she immediately knew what was on my mind. She got up, grabbed my hand and led me to a tree, where we got quite frisky while staring across the horizon. After enjoying our amorous play, Tania suggested that we go snorkelling, and an idea struck me. I quickly went to my bag and grabbed something. Then I waded in the sea and, as Tania was snorkelling, showed her the ring underwater. It sparkled and shone beautifully, glinting off the sun. The white gold band was a striking contrast against the sand, and the diamond looked huge submerged! I couldn't have planned a more perfect marriage proposal. Tania was awestruck as she gaped back at me. "Yes!" she burst out and kissed me deeply, making that day the most romantic, brilliant and blissful one of my life. That trip to South America was incredible, and I love reminiscing about those memories. Cherishing that day was a wonderful way to pass the time while running yesterday.

Thursday, 23 March 2017

Yesterday, London was attacked by a terrorist. The man ploughed through Westminster Bridge with his car, killing two people and injuring dozens more. He then crashed into the gate of the Houses of Parliament, got out and stabbed to death an unarmed police officer before being shot dead by another officer. It was terrible, sad, horrific news. On my run today I was thinking about how we could stop this awful violence. I was also concerned about other terrorist attacks that might happen in the future, especially during the Paris Marathon, where the likelihood of an attack is probably greater, given that it would be a mass-participation event, and Paris has been targeted by terrorists in the past. Obviously, I'm concerned about my family's safety because they will be there to cheer me on. However, I had to push these thoughts out of my head because if I start getting scared and continually fear for my safety, that would be giving in to the terrorists and allowing them to win. I think making us afraid is exactly what the terrorists want; they want to instil fear in us and change the way we live. But I think that one way to fight them is to show them that they will not win, and we will not be cowed by their actions. We will be defiant and condemn the attacks, but we will carry on living normally to show them that their actions are futile.

I wasn't sure if going for a run was smart, considering that I'm still not well. My fever broke on Monday night, but it was replaced by a stomach bug. I've got a bad case of diarrhoea, and couldn't keep anything down over the past two days. This morning was better, but I still felt weak. However, after three days off, I needed to get outside and stretch my legs. I've only missed a day of training so far this week, so it wasn't too bad, and having several days' rest was probably useful for my muscles and my Achilles tendon. But I'm sure being sick and not keeping any food down affected my overall fitness. Indeed, starting the run, I was terribly weak. I didn't push it hard and kept it fairly easy, so by the end, I felt more energised. The marathon is fast approaching, so I have to stay healthy until then.

While I was ill, I thought about how awful it would be if we got sick on Kilimanjaro. I wondered if it would be possible for me to walk if I get a fever, and how I could continue climbing with a temperature. Eventually I just shrugged the thought from my head and fell asleep. I just prayed that Tania and I both stay healthy for our climb.

Monday, 27 March 2017

So I lost an hour of sleep today due to the clocks going forward over the weekend. I'd planned to get up early and do a swim after I dropped off Elisa, but I couldn't get out of bed. This was partly due to daylight savings time, and partly to Elisa keeping us awake again. I was so tired this morning, I had to give swimming a miss and rearrange my training schedule for the week. I did a run today instead and planned a swim on Wednesday. Over the years I've learned to be flexible with my training because I know that life will always throw curveballs my way. Obviously, the key to a successful training programme is not to miss too many sessions.

Paris is two weeks away, so I'm entering the taper phase of my marathon training. The idea is to strengthen my body through more rest rather than adding workouts. The taper period will start gradually because the training that I do still counts; however, the workload will decrease. Today was just a short interval session, although it wasn't easy. I know interval sets are supposed to be hard, but my breathing was more strained and my stride heavier than usual. I'm not too worried, but I'm conscious of my health. With the race less than two weeks away, in theory, I should be nearly at my peak fitness. But for some reason, today's run was sluggish and I can tell that my performance has dropped. Perhaps it's the lingering effects of being sick, and I'll gain my full fitness in the next few days.

Thursday, 30 March 2017

Finally, I had an enjoyable, relaxed and steady run today. I ran just over ten kilometres, and my pace was close to my intended marathon pace. I focused on my stride, and I kept my heart rate down. I wish that I can take the same pace and sensations today for the marathon next week. I can't believe that it's just around the corner. I'm getting excited, and nervous at the same time. While I was running, I kept visualising what it would be like on race day, and how I would handle different situations. It's important to rehearse the race as much as possible during training; that way I'm prepared for certain scenarios if they come up. For example, I visualised how I would replenish my water bottle. It might sound simple, but filling up a bottle while running is trickier than it sounds. When I ran the Manchester Marathon last year, I carried a small running bottle. I also took electrolyte tablets and dropped one in the bottle every time I filled it up. I'd learned that you could lose as much as 1.5 litres of fluid per hour while sweating and that you need to replenish the salt that you loose with your sweat. Taking electrolytes to replace the salt helped prevent my legs cramping.

There is nothing worse than getting a cramp during a run, and it was a hard lesson to learn, especially during my first marathon: the 2008 Amsterdam Marathon. That was a momentous year since it was the year Sofia was born; plus I did my first triathlon, which was a sprint-distance race. Back then, I didn't know much about race nutrition and my training was more ad hoc as I didn't follow any plan. The main thing I focused on when training for my first marathon was changing my running style. In 2008, I discovered a book called *ChiRunning* by Danny Dreyer, which advocated using more of your core muscles and allowing gravity to help propel you forward. That book completely changed my running style, allowing me to go faster with less pain after long runs. I still practise it today, and recommend it to most runners when we discuss improving our technique. Back in 2008, when I was training for Amsterdam, I concentrated on applying the ChiRunning method. I foolishly ignored the other aspect of training – race nutrition.

The first twelve kilometres of the race went by fast – due to my inexperience, too fast. I set out way too quickly and didn't drink enough; a common rookie mistake. Just before the halfway point, both my calves started cramping. It was a nightmare scenario, and I was walking before I even reached the half-marathon point. By the time the cramps went away, my calves hurt so much that I could barely run. At one point I was ready to call it a day, but I was on a part of the course where there were no marshals or race officials around. So I was forced to carry on until the next drinks station, and by that time, my morale had picked up, and I managed to continue. After about four hours and fifty minutes, I eventually crossed the finish line. It was one of the most painful races that I had ever done, and I remember crying for what seemed like hours afterwards. I let all of the emotions pass through me, and it was an incredibly powerful feeling.

Finishing the Amsterdam Marathon was special, and I will never forget that moment. The fact that Tania also ran her first half-marathon that day made it more memorable. After I finished, I stayed by the finishing chute, bawling my eyes out while I waited for her. It was phenomenal seeing her cross the line, and we were able to share such a huge accomplishment together. We celebrated the following day with a long fat spliff in one of Amsterdam's famous cafes. I remember hobbling into the place, but the joint helped relax my muscles, so that I was walking almost normally when we got to the airport later that evening.

It would be another eight years before I attempted my second marathon. Last year I ran the 2016 Manchester Marathon, which was terrific mostly due to the route being pancake flat. Plus, I had a lot more knowledge about training and race nutrition – namely, drinking more fluids with electrolytes and taking gels to replenish my body's glycogen store to fuel my muscles. My training went well, and I proudly finished the race in three hours and fifty-eight minutes: a massive improvement on my Amsterdam time. I'm not aiming for a personal best in Paris, but it would be perfect if I could run it in under four hours. Either way, I hope that things go well on race day and that I don't encounter any huge problems like I did in Amsterdam. I want to enjoy chasing that smile for the whole 42.2 kilometres.

Monday, 03 April 2017

Houston, we have a problem! I woke up on Saturday with a weird pain in my left Achilles tendon, and it hurts when I lift up my heel. I can feel it when walking, or going up and down the stairs. When I tried to run, the pain was still there, so I decided it was best to stop. It was strange because my last run was last Thursday and I did it fairly easily. I didn't notice anything on Friday, and so I couldn't figure out what had happened or how I could've injured it. Tania's brother and his family were visiting from Spain; they arrived last Friday. We did some sightseeing and wandered around Central London, but apart from walking, I did nothing strenuous that could've aggravated my Achilles. The only thing I could think of that may have caused it was when Elisa was sitting on my lap on the Tube, and I was bouncing her by lifting my heel up and down. But again, I didn't sense anything at the time, so I'm perplexed as to what could have caused the injury.

When I woke up yesterday, the pain was still there, so I didn't do my run. It was worst early in the morning, but eased off when I was walking later that day, which was encouraging but still worrying me loads. I skipped my last long run before the marathon because I didn't want to make the injury worse. After I researched it on the Internet, it seems that I may have Achilles tendinitis, and apparently the symptoms could last for three to six months! The main recommendations for non-surgical treatments are rest, ice, stretches and anti-inflammatory medication. I followed the advice and iced the area where it was hurting and took some ibuprofen. I'm trying not to panic and staying positive, but the race is this Sunday so it's hard to keep my anxiety at bay. If the pain doesn't go away, I don't know how I can run a full marathon. Also, I risk injuring it further and jeopardising the Kilimanjaro climb and the Outlaw Triathlon. To calm myself, I put these thoughts out of my mind and put together a plan for this week. I figured the best thing to do is rest it as much as possible, and pray the pain will go away by Sunday. I might do an easy swim to keep my fitness level up, and perhaps an easy cycle to see how pedalling affects it. Then I'll attempt an easy test run on Thursday and assess the situation from there.

The pain today is not as bad as yesterday, and I contemplated doing an easy swim but decided against it. For now, I'll take it day by day and hope that I'm fine by this Sunday.

Wednesday, 05 April 2017

I am extremely relieved that the pain in my Achilles seems to have gone away. I told Tania my plan of going out for a test run, but she thought that I should stay off it until the marathon on Sunday. However, I was itching to get out there and see how my Achilles would feel. My body is so used to exercise that, after a few days off, it's as if I'm going through withdrawal and I'm desperately craving a run. Perhaps it was all psychological, but I decided that today would be a perfect day to go for an easy run and see how it goes.

Sofia is on Easter break, so I had to take her with me. It was timely, because it meant that I couldn't run too fast. The original plan was that she would ride her bike alongside me. However, since the garage is still not fully renovated – don't get me started on the extremely slow builders – her bike was not easily accessible. I had to convince her that it would be fun if she ran along with me instead of riding. After much consternation from Sofia, and a lot of pleading, prodding and encouragement from me, she grudgingly agreed.

We headed out, and I gave her some pointers about keeping her alignment straight, leaning forward, kicking back, swinging her arms and relaxed breathing – basically, all of the ChiRunning tips. I also told her to smile and have a positive attitude, and the run should be fun. However, it was pointless as she kept on stopping every ten metres, complaining of this, that and the other. I tried all the tricks in the book to keep her motivated and encourage her to continue, but she barely got moving. It's not like Sofia is unfit; I know full well that she was capable of running with me, and I had set a slow pace that I knew she would be comfortable with. However, she didn't want to do it, so it was like pulling teeth to get her to move. After about 2.5 kilometres and a lot of walking, I decided it was best to stop before I completely lost my patience. I had to remind myself that she is only nine after all and probably hasn't run any further than a hundred metres. So I gave her a tight hug and told her she did well for having a go. As we walked home, I noticed that there was no pain in my Achilles at all, so it seems whatever it was had healed itself.

Today was probably my last run – if I can even call it that – before the marathon. I'm feeling fit and rested, plus extremely relieved that my Achilles tendon seems to be okay. I have to ensure that I eat properly for the next few days, and perhaps do some light stretches. Last Sunday, my friend completed the Manchester Marathon and obliterated his target time. His main goal was 3:59:59 and he finished in three hours and forty-six minutes. Someone I know from Parkrun also ran, and did even better, completing the 42.2-kilometre course in three hours and twenty-seven minutes! I'm extremely happy for both of them for achieving their goals and doing so well. I hope my race will be just as well.

I checked the weather forecast for Paris on Sunday, and it's going to be sunny with a high of 23°C. This is way hotter than any of my training runs, which concerns me. This morning, for example, it was only 7°C and chilly. So I'll have to remember to keep cool and drink a lot more on race day. I'm also planning to take a gel every twenty-five minutes as opposed to every thirty minutes like I did last year when I ran the Manchester Marathon. My pace last year dropped at around the thirty-two-kilometre mark, and I think it was due to using up all of my gels. I'm also planning on bringing a lot more electrolyte tablets, which I will add to my water bottle. Hopefully, they will give out small bottles at the water stations, so it will be easy for me to pour it into my running bottle. Visualising this should pay off. However, if they hand out water in cups it will be trickier. It might even be worthwhile to stop and fill up my running bottle as opposed to doing it while running. In any case, it's important that I at least rehearse all this in my mind so that I know what to do on race day. Tonight and tomorrow, I need to prepare for the trip and plan the other logistics for the race. Since we're flying to Paris, it's going to take more preparation than usual, especially as we have the kids to organise as well. We're meeting up with a good friend whom I haven't seen in almost five years, so I'm excited for that, and for our kids to meet each other. But I must stay away from alcohol, which would probably put a damper on things. I have to stay strong and not throw away months of training by getting carried away and getting drunk with an old friend.

Tuesday, 11 April 2017

Last Thursday night, just before I started packing for Paris, I thought that in five days' time I would be back home, sitting at my desk, and the whole weekend would be just another experience that I can relive in my memory. Now, five days later, reliving those memories is probably no different from imagining something that hasn't happened – with the exception that this actually did happen, and I have photos to prove it. Plus, I'm sure that the pain I'm currently experiencing is real and not just a figment of my imagination. So, before the weekend's events become a distant memory, I will try to recount most of what happened.

It was timely that Sofia was off from school, so the girls were able to cheer me on and we had a mini family holiday out during the weekend in Paris. We caught a 6am flight on Friday, which Tania complained about. She kept asking why we hadn't booked the Eurostar instead. A 6am flight meant leaving the house at around 4am, so we both knew that it was going to be a long day with two tired kids. I aimed to get my packing done on the Thursday afternoon so that I could get to bed early, but, as usual, by the time we got the girls' stuff ready and got them to bed, it was already past ten, and I hadn't even started packing my stuff. Then I updated my JustGiving page and reminded my friends of the upcoming marathon, hoping to get more donations for Cancer Research. It was past midnight by the time I finished, and just when I was finally drifting to sleep, the alarm went off and it was time to get up again.

The flight itself was straightforward enough, and the girls were excited. Travelling with Elisa was getting easier too, and Tania and I debated whether we should bring the pushchair or just her scooter. In the end, we decided on the pushchair, which was the right decision considering the amount of walking that we did throughout the weekend. The flight was a short hop, and it was early morning by the time we got to our hotel. It was too early to check in, so we just dropped off our bags and started wandering around Paris. It was a beautiful sunny day, and more like summertime as opposed to spring. We walked along the River Seine up to Notre Dame Cathedral, and then to Luxembourg Gardens, where Sofia and Elisa took in a pony ride. At that point, we were all getting tired, so I suggested that we do my race registration and then head back to the hotel.

Registering, I was slightly anxious when I had to show my GP's letter instead of the standard medical certificate. The first person I presented it to took one look at it and immediately shook her head and called over a colleague, but it turned out that she was getting someone who could read English. The next person took the letter and examined it for what seemed like a long time; understandably because English was probably not his first language. After some consternation while he made sure that it contained the correct wording, he eventually stamped it and handed it back to me, which was a relief. The process was actually relatively straightforward. I've been to other race expos before, so I knew what to expect. Usually, there would be a lot of exhibitors wanting to sell you stuff, so I didn't want to linger. But we stayed for a while because Sofia insisted on getting as much free stuff as possible. Sadly, she was disappointed because she only managed to get a few pins, some flags and a couple of stick-on tattoos. Eventually, we all got fed up and just wanted to go back to the hotel and get some rest. When we got there, we relaxed for a bit before heading out to get an early dinner.

It was torturous to be in France and have to watch what I ate. I knew that I should be carb-loading, but all the delicious items on the menu were tempting. In the end, I couldn't resist and settled for some escargots to start and a mushroom risotto. The restaurant that Tania picked had good reviews, but sadly we were all disappointed with the food. Tania and I joked that the reviews must've been 'fake news'. However, we had a pleasant dining experience, and I especially enjoyed the girls being grossed out by watching me eat snails.

When we got back to the hotel, our room was boiling. We called the front desk and explained the situation, and they said that we should turn off the thermostat fan because the hotel heater was on instead of the air conditioning. The receptionist explained that it was unusually hot and technically still springtime; hence they still had the heating on because the nights could get chilly. So I turned off the thermostat and opened the window, but it was no use. We were all so hot that it was hard to get any sleep. Despite being extremely tired, I woke up several times, sweating profusely. I'm sure the lack of a decent night's rest was a factor in my race performance.

The next day, we met up with my old uni friend. Coincidentally, we'd done our first half-marathon together back in 2002. That was the first running race I ever entered. I remember passing him in the last few kilometres, and we joked that it was probably the reason why he never ran another race again. It was nice to see him and his family and catch up on old times. They showed us around Paris, and we did a lot more walking. But much as I would've liked to go to a pub and savour some drinks, we managed to resist the urge and eventually said goodbye in the afternoon. That was timely because I was keen to get an early night for the marathon the following day. In the evening, we had an early dinner at an Italian restaurant so that I could have a bowl of pasta to carb-load. The girls love pasta, and they commented that the sauce was almost equal to their nonno's sauce. After dinner, it was back to the hotel to start preparing and organising my gear for the race.

Since I didn't have to worry about swimming or cycling, there was a lot less kit to worry about. The only things I needed were my running shoes, running socks, spandex shorts to avoid chafing, running shorts, running T-shirt, heart-rate monitor, GPS watch, race belt, race number, running bottle, and gels and electrolyte tablets for nutrition. That might sound like a lot, but a small fraction compared to a triathlon. I also organised the small bag that I would use to carry my phone and an extra T-shirt that I would need to keep warm on the way to the race.

Once I finished packing and organising my gear, I read through the race information one more time and planned where to meet Tania. After some online research, we concluded that the best place for them to watch me was from the Place de la

Bastille. This vantage point was a short walk from our hotel; plus the race route would pass close to it twice: once around the five-kilometre point and then back again just after the half-marathon mark of twenty-one kilometres. We decided that it would be easier for them to not bother coming to the finish line because of the huge crowds. It would've been hard to drag Sofia and Elisa up and down the Métro stairs with that many people around, so the best thing was for them to catch me at the five- and twenty-one-kilometre mark and then they could relax. I would meet them back at the hotel after I finished.

Having run a marathon last year helped a huge amount. I had experience on my side, plus confidence that I had completed the distance before. I also knew what to expect, so the night before, I rehearsed the race day from waking up all the way to the starting line. First, I double-checked my start time and then subtracted an hour-and-a-quarter to give me the time I should arrive at the venue. I needed enough time to find the bag drop-off point and make my way to the starting line without having to rush. Once I knew the time that I would need to be at the venue, I calculated the amount of time to get there so I would know when I needed to leave the hotel. Once I knew that, I subtracted about an hour-and-a-half to determine the time I would need to wake up, and therefore set my alarm for. Going through that process put me at ease, so I knew that I had plenty of time to get ready. It was important to be organised so that I didn't waste any energy panicking or rushing in the morning. Plus, should anything unexpected happen, I would have enough time to deal with it.

After mentally rehearsing what I needed to do in the morning, organising my stuff and planning the meeting point with Tania, there was nothing left to do but go to sleep. However, our room was still boiling, even though we had asked for a fan to be sent up. The fan did cool the room a tiny bit, but it was so loud that it woke me throughout the night.

When I woke up on Sunday morning, it was just a matter of going through the motions and doing what I had visualised doing. The whole thing went exactly as I'd rehearsed it, and the next thing I knew, I found myself in a Métro carriage full of runners. The excitement and anxiety in the air were palpable, but I didn't feel either. I got chatting with an Irish man who wasn't carrying anything but a large bottle of water. He commented on how hot it was and asked me how I planned to deal with it. I explained my plan of taking a gel every twenty-five minutes and carrying a 330-millilitre running bottle, which I planned to refill at every stop and mix with an electrolyte tablet. He stared at me, looking a bit distressed, and confessed that he had not thought about race nutrition or hydration at all. I backtracked and reassured him that he would be all right, but I wasn't convincing. I think I scared him away, because he jumped out two stops before where the organisers had suggested we get off.

When I exited the Charles de Gaulle-Étoile Métro station, the first thing I noticed was the Arc de Triomphe. What a magnificent monument, and it gave me an immediate buzz. Excitement rushed through me, and I was eager to get going. But before going to the start line, I needed to find the bag drop-off point. I'd thought there would be signs everywhere directing runners where to go, but there was nothing. It was the only part of the whole weekend for which the organisation was poor. I double-checked the race pack, but found no directions, and there were no signs anywhere. I went around asking several runners, but most didn't know either. Luckily, I came across an Australian who knew where to go, so I followed him. We got chatting, and he told me that it would be his second marathon. I asked him what his first had been and he replied that it was an ultramarathon. It turned out that he'd run the Marathon des Sables the previous year! This is arguably the hardest race in the world: a six-day, 251-kilometre ultramarathon, which is approximately the distance of six regular marathons. It is held every year in the Sahara Desert, and participants have to carry their food for the whole duration. All of my previous race achievements paled in comparison and I gave him serious respect. I joked that the Paris Marathon would be just a training run for him. He laughed, and we wished each other luck as we separated on finding our bag drop-off area.

I managed to work out the weird numbering system the French used, dropped off my bag and made my way to the start line for my start wave. At that point, all I thought about was the heat, and that I had to remember to keep drinking. The forecast for the day was 24°C, and when I looked up there wasn't a cloud in the sky. Normally, the glorious bright sunny day would be perfect holiday weather, but not for running a marathon; especially for someone who lives in London and had been training under the grey English skies in temperatures that barely reached double digits. I had neither trained nor accounted for hot weather. I recounted my gels and double-checked my electrolyte tablets, wishing that they would be enough to get me around the course.

As the volunteers opened the gate to let our wave in towards the starting line, I was overcome by excitement, and happiness. I took a few seconds, closed my eyes and gave gratitude for making it to the starting line. I knew that just getting there was an achievement in itself, and as I looked around, I had huge admiration and respect for all the runners around me. Most of us had taken enormous amount of time and sacrificed a lot just to be there. I could sense the camaraderie, and I genuinely wished that all of us would have a good race and achieve our goals. I loved that moment just before the race began; it seemed like we were one army ready to do battle. We were all united, and we all gave a giant cheer when they started the countdown.

Three, two, one, and with a shout I started my Paris Marathon journey. I jogged until I crossed the timing mats, then pressed start on my watch, and I was off. My strategy was quite simple: I would break down the race into five-kilometre chunks. To run under four hours, I would need to set a pace of around 5:37/km. With that speed, I calculated that every five kilometres should take me roughly twenty-eight minutes. After each kilometre, I assessed my pace and made sure that I was within target. I also focused on making sure that my stride was relaxed. Along with reminding myself to keep taking sips from my water bottle. I also concentrated on the people around me and the ground immediately in front of me, so I didn't trip on anything. With so many things to think about, the run was mentally demanding. How can people say running is boring?

During the first two kilometres, I made sure that I was fairly relaxed, and tried to keep my heart rate down. However, the sun was already hot, and I sought to get some shade. But it was futile because most of the other runners were doing the same, and it was impossible for all of us to run on the same stretch of tarmac. Eventually we turned a corner, and there was nowhere to hide from the sunlight. In hindsight, it would've been a good idea to wear a hat. After another kilometre, I found myself just behind the four-hour pacesetter. I figured that I would stay behind him for as long as possible and aim to finish around four hours. My pace still felt fairly relaxed, but when I checked my watch, I was shocked to find that my heart rate was in Zone 4.8! That was way above my cruising zone. I tried to relax by slowing my breathing, and I drank more, but it was no use. My heart rate remained high, which I guessed was due to the heat. I tried not to think about it and maintained the pace, until my watch alarm went off to remind me that it had been twenty-five minutes. Time to take my first gel. I grabbed one that I taped on my water bottle, ripped off the packet with my teeth and enjoyed the sweet berry flavour to give me a boost, knowing that I was nearing the first five-kilometre mark. Tania and the girls would be around, so I started scanning for them in the crowd. We'd agreed that I'd run on the right side of the course and they would stand on the same side so that it would be easier for us to see each other. But after passing the five-kilometre sign, there was no sign of them. I kept looking around for another kilometre but had no luck, so I kept my head down and just focused on running. I thought that I must've missed them and started to feel bad; then all of a sudden I heard this tiny voice scream, "Daddy!" I looked up in time to see Tania and then Sofia and Elisa waving tiny Union Jack and Maple Leaf flags. I had just enough time to give Tania a high five before running past them. I wanted to stop and run back to kiss them, but it was still early in the race, and I was swept up with the river of runners behind me. It was impossible for me to stop, but seeing them was enough. I beamed, with love and pure joy surging through me. I was on a high, and it carried me for miles. I kept replaying Sofia's squeaky voice through the crowd, and it seemed to lift my feet.

Despite the heat, the kilometres seemed to go by and the crowd support was fantastic. However, I was very aware of how hot the sun was, and made sure that I kept on drinking. Towards the half-marathon point, my energy level started to drop. My pace was still fine, but there were one or two kilometres where I knew that I was off the pace. After the third water stop, I watched the four-hour pacesetter flag slowly run away from me and I knew that I had slowed down. I wasn't worried and tried to convince myself that I could still run around four hours. At around the twenty-one-kilometre point, I started scanning for Tania and the girls again. I saw them in the distance and I pulled over to give Tania a quick kiss and Sofia a high five. That gave me another boost. However, at that point, I knew that going under four hours was no longer the target. I did the half-marathon in about two hours and two minutes; it was impossible for me to go under four hours due to the heat. At that moment, I felt that finishing would be enough of a challenge. I was still running well, but the heat was melting my energy away.

As my pace started to slow, we entered a long, dark tunnel; it seemed that the only light came from glow-in-the-dark balloons on either side. I thought the tunnel would give us some respite from the heat, but it was more like entering a sauna. I didn't like that section of the course at all, and what got me through it was this wave of sound that all the runners made. It was like doing the Mexican wave at sporting events, but instead of seeing the wave, I could hear and feel a wave of sound go past me and continue down the tunnel. It was a unique experience and pretty cool.

When I emerged from the tunnel, I was blinded by the sun. The uphill climb to street level was torturous. I can't remember exactly which part of the race that was, but looking at my splits on my GPS watch afterwards, it must've been around the twenty-five- or twenty-six-kilometre mark. That was the point where I started to slow down and, in doing so, my stride changed. I shortened it, which must have caused my feet to impact the ground harder, and this started a downwards spiral. I also ran out of water at that point, and the water station was still about two kilometres away. My legs started to cramp, so I slowed down even further. As I reached the water station, I stopped running and walked for the first time to fill up my bottle. I was around the twenty-nine-kilometre mark. I thought that there was no way my legs could do the remaining distance. To banish these negative thoughts, I concentrated on breaking down the race into smaller chunks and switched to focusing on two kilometres at a time. I just had to run for two kilometres, then maybe take a break. That seemed doable, and I managed to start running again. I saw other runners suffering from the heat as I realised my water bottle was empty. I ran towards someone in the crowd and asked for a sip of theirs. That wasn't enough and I was desperate, so I started looking around for discarded bottles that might have some water left in them. I managed to find two on the ground, and got a few sips from them. It was that bad.

But despite all of this, I managed to continue, and by the time I passed the forty-kilometre mark, every step was pure agony. My leg muscles were being shredded with each stride. But at that point, there was no more stopping, and I committed to running until the finish line. Finally, I rounded the corner onto Avenue Foch and saw the finishing banner; then everything was a blur. I remember the pain, the joy, the excitement and finally the pure relief of crossing the line. I shouted to release all my emotions, and raised my arms in triumph! I looked down to stop my watch and my time was 4:33:26. A hint of disappointment passed through me; then I thought, *sometimes you don't chase the smile; you let it come to you.* Then the endorphins surged through my body and bliss washed over me. The smile on my face felt brighter than the sun, and I felt like hugging everyone. The sense of accomplishment was immense.

Eventually, I composed myself and walked back to get my bag. I collected my medal, finisher's T-shirt, extra bottles of water and some recovery food along the way. As soon as I got my bag, I sat down and immediately called Tania. Hearing her voice felt similar to crossing the finish line, and I almost broke down crying. It was intense joy, and I just wanted to share it with her. I knew that I couldn't have done it without Tania's support; she and the girls were an enormous part of my accomplishment. All I wanted to do was get back to the hotel and give them a massive hug. But I had to wait a while to give my body a chance to recover. I stretched and watched the stream of finishers limp by and shared knowing smiles with some of them.

I struggled getting back to the hotel, and negotiating all of the stairs on the Métro was painful. It was almost as tough as the marathon itself. When I finally walked into our hotel room, it felt the same as finishing the race. My reward was the massive hugs from the girls. Elisa's face lit up when she saw my medal, and I put it around her neck. She then started jumping up and down, saying, "Daddy is the winner, Daddy is the champion!" I didn't correct her; I just sat back to relish the moment. After a couple of hours' rest and a nice shower, plus some ibuprofen, we were all out and about again. As much as I would've liked to just curl up and sleep, I also wanted to go out and do some sightseeing with my family. So we went and saw the Eiffel Tower, and then walked back towards the Arc de Triomphe. To celebrate, we stopped at a charming restaurant where I tucked into a tender, juicy steak. When we got back to the hotel, I went online to post an update about the marathon and was delighted to find out that a few friends had made some large donations. My fundraising total had gone from £260 all the way up to £722, so I'm close to reaching my goal of £1,000. I couldn't be any more grateful for all the support and encouragement from my friends. All I could do was repeat my mantra: "Life is good. Thank you, thank you, thank you."

Our flight home the following day was not until 10pm, so we had a whole day of sightseeing. When I woke up, it seemed like a bus had hit me. My calves and quads were completely shredded, and it was a real struggle to walk. However, I couldn't have stayed in the hotel room even if I'd wanted to, because we had to check out. So I forced myself to get up and see the Paris landmarks. I don't know if it was intentional or not, but Tania decided to check out Sacré-Cœur first, where they found it hilarious watching me go up and down the million steps of the basilica. Then we continued walking and hit all of the major tourist attractions including the Moulin Rouge, the Louvre and others. I couldn't believe how much we walked; my watch said that we did over eleven kilometres! And it was a day after I'd run a marathon. But I wasn't the only one; along the way I saw fellow runners hobbling along with their loved ones, all struggling to see as much of the City of Love as possible. In the end, I was glad that we did some more sightseeing because we all enjoyed it as a family. We had a fabulous time, and I'm sure it's a holiday we won't forget. I certainly won't.

Back in London, I'm still in a daze; I'm sure because my whole body is terribly sore from the incredibly tough effort it took to finish! The sense of accomplishment and elation from completing a tough challenge are overcoming my extreme tiredness. The next few days will be recovery – I don't have any choice. My legs are still in pain, and stairs are my enemy. I'm optimistic that by Friday it should be back to normal and I can get on the bike or do some swimming. Now that I've finished my first challenge, my training will focus on the Ironman. One down, two to go. Bring on Kilimanjaro next – *allez, allez, allez!*

Arc de Triomphe Selfie

THE WHISKY ROUTE

Monday, 17 April 2017

My recovery is going pretty well. My legs were sore till about last Thursday, and it was agony walking up and down the stairs. Sitting down and getting up wasn't fun either. By Friday my legs finally felt normal, and I was able to go for an easy ride. I did about forty kilometres, and took it fairly easily, but somehow I managed to pass a lot of people. I was astonished, as normally people would overtake me, so either my fitness had picked up and my legs had got stronger, or there were just slower people riding that day. Perhaps it was the latter because it was the Easter bank holiday, so Friday was a day off. The ride was pleasant, and I even took some selfies with the giraffes and zebras at London Zoo.

The following day, Tania and I went on our toughest hike yet: a fifteen-kilometre loop around Box Hill in the Surrey countryside. It was a beautiful day for a hike, and it was lovely to spend the whole day with just the two of us. There was a significant amount of climbing involved, as we went over five hills, with a total elevation gain of about 508 metres. Tania set a fairly fast pace, and powered through all of the hills. My quads haven't fully recovered from the marathon, so I took it a lot slower. We both felt strong during and after the climb. It took us about four hours to complete the loop, but we weren't as tired as our previous date hike, so our fitness had improved since then.

I took yesterday off because it was Easter. We spent the day at Tania's parents' and had an Easter meal with the family. Tania's dad is an excellent cook and, being Italian, cooks the best Italian food: so delicious that we rarely go to Italian restaurants anymore because restaurant food doesn't quite live up to his. The only problem is that he loves feeding people, so every time we visit, he cooks up a feast and insists that we eat to the point that we are bursting at the seams and almost sick. Yesterday was no exception, and, since it was Easter, he gave us even more to eat, plus chocolate eggs on top. So, when I weighed myself this morning, I wasn't surprised to find my weight nearly back up to seventy kilos. With the reduced exercise during recovery, plus all the food I ate in Paris after the marathon and the Easter meal at Tania's parents', I had gained several kilos! I need to get a handle on this immediately; otherwise, it will be difficult to haul my fat ass up the mountain.

So today I went out for my first run since the marathon. I wanted to see how my legs would function after the immense effort. I started off fairly slow, and immediately my legs were sluggish. After a few minutes I stopped and stretched them out. When I got going again, it was better and I eventually immersed myself in the run. I cherished that familiar relaxation that I get when running; with each stride, I was erasing the painful memory of the marathon's last kilometres. I found it amusing how running five kilometres today was a breeze compared to the last five of the marathon. Those thirty minutes felt like an eternity, whereas today went by really quickly. It's funny how our brains perceive time and deal with adversity. After I finished running, I savoured that post-run energy, reflected on my accomplishment and was extremely thankful. *Life is good. Thank you, thank you, thank you.*

Tuesday, 18 April 2017

What a hectic and busy day. My original plan was to get in a quick hour on the turbo trainer, but it almost didn't happen. I usually try to get my workout done first thing in the morning so that it's out of the way. If I don't do it before lunchtime, most likely I won't do it at all. Even though my twelve-week Ironman training plan doesn't officially start for another two weeks, I still wanted to maintain my fitness and get stronger on the bike and in swimming. However, I'm flying to Miami on Thursday for five days. That might sound exciting, but I will be there for work mostly so I'm not sure how much free time I'll have. I'll see if I can at least do some easy runs to explore South Beach, and do some open-water swimming in the ocean. The main challenge would be not indulging in the food or getting too drunk when out with my colleagues.

Because of the upcoming trip, I had a lot of work to finish before I fly out. Plus, I'm still managing our garage build, which is still not finished. The builders are going extremely slowly and are three weeks behind schedule. Today I had to sort out replacing the water heater and shower unit that we've purchased because a friend pointed out that the advice our plumber gave us was wrong. So I had to spend a lot of time figuring out which heater would work and then exchange the old parts. Sofia was still off school – thankfully they're back tomorrow. She had decided to do her homework on the last day, and I had to spend some time helping her. To top it off, I took delivery of the sleeping bag I ordered for Kilimanjaro. I tried not to open the package because I had a lot to do, but I couldn't help myself and ended up spending quite some time checking out the sleeping bag. The bag itself looks cool, but it's bulky when packed. I suppose it needs a lot of insulation to keep us warm at −12°C. I hope it will be warm enough to do the job. Needless to say, I didn't get a chance to jump on the bike before noon.

At one o'clock we had to pick up Elisa from the nursery, so it looked even less likely that I would get a workout today. However, after getting back home, I worked hard and managed to finish all the work I needed to do. That gave me an hour before I had to drop off Sofia at her gymnastics class. I was so busy that I didn't even have time to eat anything, but I thought I should take the opportunity and eat later. After fifty minutes, I climbed off the bike drenched in sweat and satisfied that I did a workout despite my hectic day. I was proud of myself that I was productive. I was also pleased that I was disciplined and didn't skip a day. It's hard when life pulls me in so many directions; nevertheless, I managed to cope and do everything that was required of me. I know for a lot of people juggling the work-life balance is hard enough, so finding the time to train for an Ironman seems almost impossible. I guess this is part of the challenge, and it takes dedication and commitment to achieve it. I need to maintain it, and be as prepared as I can be when I get to that starting line.

Wednesday, 19 April 2017

I fly out to Miami tomorrow, and last night I finished the work that I needed to complete before leaving. So I had time for a long swim and a quick run today. I was energised because of the lighter recovery workouts that I'd been doing, so today I went to the pool and did my longest swim so far: 3.6 kilometres, and it took me an hour and twenty minutes of moving time, and if I include the time resting between sets, the elapsed time was an hour and thirty-three minutes. I swam back and forth for ninety-seven laps, or 194 lengths in total. Sometimes it even boggles me, the distances I'm doing for the Ironman training. Some people can't even run for over an hour, let alone swim for that amount of time. It just goes to show how much I've progressed with my swimming, and that I'm capable of swimming that far without becoming exhausted. To prove the point, I went for an easy six-kilometre run afterwards to see how my legs were after the swim. I found that they were fine, and the run was relaxing.

I know swimming in open water is very different to swimming in a pool, but today's swim added to my confidence. I'm glad to do two solid sessions today because I'm not sure how much exercise I can do in Miami. But I'm looking forward to swimming in the ocean.

Sunday, 30 April 2017

My training this past week was disrupted by general day-to-day life, and I'm glad that the week is finally over. Miami was excellent, but coming home was tiring and interrupted most of my training. Although, I didn't intend to follow any particular plan for a couple of weeks after the Paris Marathon. I knew I needed a couple of weeks to recover, so I planned to do more ad-hoc workouts as opposed to following a specific programme.

After checking into my hotel, I immediately went for a walk to explore the beach. The hotel was only two blocks from the beach, so it wasn't far. I flew with my colleagues and we arrived in the afternoon after a nine-and-a-half-hour flight, so I had several hours to lie on the sand and stretch my legs. It was sunny and hot, but windy, and the sea looked rough. I thought about jumping in, but the choppy waves scared me off, so I decided that I would rather go for a run. The sun gave me a big surge of energy and I was exhilarated, especially after being cooped up in an aeroplane on a long transatlantic flight. I ran along the South Beach boardwalk with the wide beach on one side, and tall high-rises on the other. It was a refreshing way to explore the city, and I absorbed the new scenery. I wore my Paris Marathon finisher's T-shirt, to show off my accomplishment. Most didn't pay any attention to me, but there were a couple of runners who did notice the shirt and gave me knowing smiles. That slight recognition was enough to make me giddy and I pushed my pace a fraction faster. I guess that's why we wear our finisher's T-shirts like badges of honour: so that we can parade our success for others to see, wanting some recognition for the effort and sacrifice that went into obtaining them. Incidentally, I picked up two T-shirts after Paris because I want to show them off as often as possible. I know it was bad form, but in the heat of the moment and the high of just completing the marathon I didn't care, so I took two knowing full well that I intended to boast about my achievement to the general running community as often as possible.

I was energised after running five kilometres, and thought that it would tire me out so that I would get adequate sleep, but that wasn't the case. I had a scheduled team dinner with all my colleagues and some clients. It was entertaining, and I ended up drinking quite a few Cuba libres. We got back to the hotel very late, and I immediately passed out. But after a couple of hours, I was suddenly woken by a loud beeping from the hallway. I didn't know what it was, but it lasted for at least half an hour. Eventually, I managed to fall back to sleep, but woke up after an hour sweating buckets because I was too hot. I then remembered that when I'd got back my room had felt as cold as the Antarctic, so I must have turned off the air conditioning. I got up and fiddled around with the thermostat, which was in Fahrenheit, so I had no concept at all of what the temperature was. Eventually, I managed to turn the air conditioning on, and went back to bed. It was only quarter to five in the morning, so I attempted to go back to sleep but my brain was fully awake and couldn't. I guess my body clock was still set to London time. That first night I only got about three hours' sleep, and, to my dismay, that pattern was repeated for the whole trip.

The following day I managed to run another five kilometres assuming that it would again energise me. But with the lack of sleep, plus the alcohol in my system, I found that run more draining. Thankfully, I had most of the morning to lie on the beach and nap under the sun. Most of the weekend was spent working on our seminar, so I didn't have any time to go running.

Our flight back was last Monday night, so I went for another five-kilometre run. The sea was a lot calmer that day, and I also went for a swim. I had thought about taking my wetsuit to Miami, but I was glad I didn't because the water was so warm I probably would've overheated. It was fantastic swimming in open water as opposed to going up and down the pool. I focused on my sighting and made sure that I was swimming in a straight line. Obviously, there are no lane markers in open water, so sighting is a crucial skill. What you do is look up once in a while and use reference points like buoys or the shoreline in order to swim straight. It is a weak point of mine, and in the races that I entered in previous years, I must have swum an extra couple of hundred metres because I swam in zigzags. So last year I developed a better technique when we were on holiday in Greece. I incorporated sighting every third stroke before breathing on my left side. What I do is look up just above the water to see my reference point before rolling my head to the side to inhale with my mouth. I practised the same technique in Miami, and it worked. I picked buoys as targets along the way, and I hit most of them. When I looked at the map after uploading my swim data from my GPS watch, the line was a lot straighter compared to the squiggles from previous open-water swims. This boosted my confidence.

On that last day in Miami, while sitting on the beach, I reminisced about backpacking in Thailand. I initially set out with three guys from Canada. Two of them I knew from university, and at the time we were working on a project together. The other guy was a friend of theirs. I had told them about my travels in Oz and convinced them to check out Thailand with me. But when we landed in Bangkok, I immediately realised that

I wanted to travel on my own. I'd been alone towards the end of my Australia trip and I loved it, and I thought it would be better if I set off by myself in Thailand. Partly because it was the other guys' first time backpacking and I didn't want to influence their experience by trying to relive the same experiences I'd had with my friends in Australia; but mainly, I thought it would be more exciting to explore the country on my own, meeting new people and making new friends along the way. That decision proved to be the right one, and I cherished every minute I spent in that beautiful country. I learned a lot about myself, and didn't mind keeping my own company. Plus I did manage to meet a lot of people, especially my great friend Caroline.

I was in Koh Samui when I met Caroline and her sister, and the three of us spent months together in our tiny wooden huts on an idyllic beach in Maenam. We spent our days playing cards, smoking spliffs, reading books and lounging in our hammocks. It was paradise, and I made it last for as long as possible. I managed to stretch a one-month trip into three months, the majority of the time just chilling on that beach with Caroline and her sister. But eventually, reality came calling, and I had to go back home to Canada. The following year, when I went to London, I stayed at Caroline's place for a few weeks, and she helped me get settled in the UK. She introduced me to Tania, one of her best friends from university, and the rest, as they say, is history. Caroline is a dear friend, and she's a significant part of our lives. She was the maid of honour at our wedding, and she's Sofia's godmother. Meeting new people is one of the best things about travelling, and when I was in Thailand, I was always with the company of other backpackers. However, sitting on the beach in Miami I thought that travelling on my own would never be the same. Now that I have a family, I just felt like I was missing something. Sitting there made me miss Tania and the girls a lot, and I wished that they were beside me enjoying the sea together.

After reminiscing about Thailand, I thought about our upcoming Kilimanjaro trip. I don't think there will be any mobile phone reception on the mountain, which won't allow us to speak to the girls for at least seven days. I can't even remember the last time I didn't talk to them for more than a day, so not hearing their voices for more than a week will be tough. It's something Tania and I will need to cope with.

As beautiful as the weather in Miami was, it was nicer coming back home to London. I didn't even mind the cool temperature that greeted me coming out of Heathrow Airport. The look on Elisa's face was priceless when I picked her up from her nursery. The same was true of Sofia when I got her from school, and she even gave me a giant hug in front of all her friends and her teacher; something that she's starting to get shy about, now that she's growing up. Lying down in my own bed was blissful, and I finally got a decent night's rest. Since I barely slept in Miami, I don't think my body ever left the UK time zone, and thankfully I didn't have jet lag. But, I was exhausted and only managed to do one session on the turbo trainer all week. I was busy managing the last of our garage renovation, which contributed to the lack of training. The builders had taken their sweet-ass time, and what should've taken six weeks is now in its tenth week! However, the end is in sight, and they will finish in the next couple of days.

Yesterday I had a solid brick session. I cycled for sixty-five kilometres around Regent's Park, followed by a four-kilometre run. The ride was steady, and I kept up with some of the faster guys. Albeit, I drafted behind and just sucked their wheels the whole time and didn't take any turns up front; still, it was brilliant to keep up with a fast group of riders. My legs felt strong, and I was glad that I hadn't lost too much fitness, even though I had been eating poorly and drinking more alcohol in the past few weeks. The run afterwards was fantastic and I was surprised by my pace. I wanted to run slowly after the cycle, but for some reason, my legs wouldn't listen and ran fast. The transition from cycling to running felt weird as usual since different muscles were being utilised. Plus, my cycling cadence was much faster than my running cadence, hence the faster pace when I started running. Getting used to the transition and making sure that I don't go too fast on the bike is something I need to work on in the coming weeks.

Today is the end of my recovery period, and tomorrow I officially start my twelve-week Ironman training plan. I haven't studied the plan properly yet, but I know it's going to take a lot more time than the marathon training. It will be another challenge to fit it into my schedule. Not to mention that our Kilimanjaro trip is a month away, and we still have a lot to do to prepare for it. Also, next weekend, Tania and I will be flying to Santorini in Greece for a friend's wedding, so that will be another disruption. But I'm not complaining. I'm grateful for everything!

Wednesday, 03 May 2017

I went out for my first long run today since the marathon, and it was excellent. I am starting my Ironman training plan, and long runs are scheduled on Wednesdays. It is going to be tricky fitting it in because of work, but I figure if I drop off the kids earlier, I should have enough time. On Tuesdays, the plan calls for a turbo session and a swim, which will be tight to squeeze into my schedule. To do both, I'll have to wake up at 6am and do the turbo before I drop off the kids. Then I plan to go straight to the pool. But yesterday was Elisa's fourth birthday, so I threw the plan out the window as we spent the morning opening her presents and playing with her new toys.

I can't believe how fast Elisa is growing up, and that she will be starting primary school in September. She got a piggy bank as one of her presents, and this morning she went around looking for some money to put in it, and inevitably asked me to give her some change. It was a good opportunity to explain to her how money works. I told her that most of the time, money has to be earned as opposed to just being given to us. To illustrate the point, I told her that if she controlled her temper and avoided whingeing all day, she could have 10p that night. I know it might seem like bribery, but it was useful to teach her a few lessons at the same time. Especially when she woke up this morning whingeing, short-tempered and just being a little brat all around. Tania tried to teach her how to be calmer by breathing instead of automatically lashing out to control her temper. I'm optimistic that my meagre incentive of earning some coins will reinforce the lesson. Parenting can be such a challenge, and I know that we don't always get it right. Sometimes, I think that an Ironman seems like a breeze compared to day-to-day parenting, which requires more stamina and determination than most sport.

I watched this film the other night called *Captain Fantastic*, which was about a dad raising his six kids in the middle of a forest away from civilisation. He and his wife homeschool their kids, as well as teach them how to survive in the wild. It was a touching film that examined several different subjects and offered an alternative idea for teaching children at home. One of the things that I took away from the film was a quote:

> *If you assume that there is no hope, you guarantee that there will be no hope. If you assume that there is an instinct for freedom, that there are opportunities to change things, then there is a possibility that you can contribute to making a better world.*
>
> (Noam Chomsky)

This resonated with me immensely, especially the first sentence. I like to think of myself as a positive person, so such quotes get me fired up and excited. I think this quote is something that I'll be using a lot in my upcoming challenges and life in general. Plus, it's something that I want to teach my kids, to follow themselves.

Tuesday, 09 May 2017

I enjoyed being back on the bike and sweating again after a couple days off. Tania and I returned from Santorini yesterday afternoon, and we had a fabulous time. Our friend's wedding was beautiful, and the island itself was just gorgeous. We were only away from Friday morning until Monday afternoon, but without the kids, it seemed like a two-week holiday. Although, I did indulge a little in the partying and got carried away with the drinking and eating, as I predicted. My training has probably been set back by at least two weeks due to the amount I drank, but I've no regrets because it was a celebration, and I can't refuse a good time.

Tania was the maid of honour and was busy helping the bride prepare, so I didn't see much of her for the first two days. However, we did get a chance to sneak out on Saturday morning, so we went for a lovely walk, which turned into a hike. We found an isolated path carved out from the cliff that led down to the sea, and followed it down. The view of the water as far as I could see was spectacular, the surrounding jagged cliffs breathtaking. We couldn't help ourselves, and got fairly amorous halfway down the path. I have to say it was probably the most beautiful place we had ever 'done it'!

The walk down was hard and slippery because of the loose dirt, which was made more difficult because we were wearing flip-flops. The climb back up got our hearts pumping, and once again reminded us of how difficult Kilimanjaro will be to climb. We chatted excitedly about having less than a month before we set off, but slightly worried at the same time about all the things we need to buy and organise before we go. However, now that Tania has finished helping her friend with the wedding, she can devote more time to the Kilimanjaro preparations.

Apart from the short hike with Tania, I did zero training while we were away. We did go to the beach for a few hours on Sunday, but I forgot my swimming goggles, so I didn't get a chance to do a proper swim. Plus, I was severely hung-over from the wedding the night before, so it was probably a bad idea anyway. Having missed a weekend from my training, I need to work hard to get it back on track. Unexpectedly, my turbo session today was alright. I thought that I would be tired due to the lack of sleep over the weekend, but I was really strong and had a solid session. The only problem was that I was also supposed to do an hour's swimming, but I didn't have enough time. I had quite a bit of work to catch up on, so it was impossible to do two sessions today. Again, finding the time to fit in all my training will be a major part of the challenge, and I need to figure it out in the coming weeks.

Wednesday, 10 May 2017

I swam steadily in the pool today for an hour and ten minutes of total moving time, with an elapsed time of an hour and seventeen minutes including all the breaks I took between sets. My watch recorded a total distance of 3,036 metres, with a pace of 2:20/100m. This is slow compared to most triathletes, but for me, good enough for my first Ironman. The important thing was that I felt completely relaxed and comfortable. It gave me confidence that swimming 3.8 kilometres is achievable. A lot of people have said that you don't win a triathlon on the swim, but you can certainly lose it in the water. For most triathletes, myself included, the swim is the weakest discipline, and for many of us, completing the swim is an achievement in itself. It was certainly the case for me when I attempted my first triathlon.

Growing up in a huge metropolis in the Philippines, I didn't have the opportunity to learn to swim. Even if my parents had had the means to send me to swimming lessons, there were no pool facilities nearby where we lived, so I never learned. When we moved to Canada just before I turned thirteen, I still didn't know how to swim. In Canada, most kids were taught at an early age, so once we settled down my parents enrolled me in classes. The only problem was that I was a complete beginner, and they put me in a class with six- and seven-year-olds – humiliating for a teenager. I only stayed to pass two levels, enough to stay afloat on my back, and I barely learned the backstroke. It wasn't enough to be completely confident in the pool. Embarrassingly, during pool parties in junior high, I had to stay in the shallow end because I didn't know how to tread water.

By the time I got to Australia in 2000, I was more confident in floating on my back and could just about put together a few strokes using the front crawl. However, the backstroke was still the only technique that I could rely on in the water. Somehow, I even managed to get my PADI diving certificate using only the backstroke, and scuba-dive in the Great Barrier Reef. For the certificate, I had to stay afloat for ten minutes and swim two hundred metres. There was no time limit for the swim, and I could use any stroke I wanted. Instead of treading water, I floated on my back, and I used the backstroke (slowly) to complete the swim. One of the things I learned in Australia was how I was more buoyant in the sea compared to the pool, which made swimming easier. That allowed me to experiment more, and I taught myself to tread water. It was a milestone for me, and added to my swimming arsenal.

When I got to Thailand in 2001, I managed to teach myself the breaststroke. The calm warm blue waters of Koh Samui were the perfect place to practise my swimming. I improved my treading water and started learning how to do the frog kick for the breaststroke. But I could only do several strokes with my head in the water, and I couldn't figure out how to breathe without stopping and treading water. Until one day when, as Caroline, her sister and I were chilling out in our hammocks, a German guy came onshore with a small sailboat. We got chatting, and he invited us onto his boat and took us out sailing. We sailed along the shore and decided to stop at a restaurant on the beach to get some drinks. But for some reason, we couldn't dock the boat on the beach, so we had to swim ashore. We were just in our swimming costumes and we had our sarongs with us that we didn't want to get wet, so we wrapped them around our heads like a turban and got in the water slowly. Without thinking about it, I just naturally started doing the breaststroke with my head above water. That was all it took; all I needed was the motivation to not get my sarong wet in order to learn how to breathe while doing the breaststroke, and from that moment it became my favourite stroke. I spent a lot of time in Thailand practising the breaststroke and treading water. I swam every day for over two months and gained a lot of confidence. From that point forward, I found that I could finally swim. Except, I still didn't know how to do the front crawl. Every time I tried, I had to stop after flailing for a couple of strokes, completely out of breath. In my head, I was still not sufficiently competent to swim long distances. I could splash about in the water, but I couldn't do it as a sporting activity.

In 2008, just before Sofia was born, I decided to sign up for my first triathlon. I entered one of the shortest distances for the sport, which was a sprint-distance event. It comprised a 750-metre swim, followed by a twenty-kilometre bike ride, finishing off with a five-kilometre run. At the time, I still couldn't swim a length of the pool with the front crawl, and therefore a triathlon seemed impossible. However, I had always wanted to learn how to swim properly, and had been fascinated by watching the sport. So I bit the bullet and signed up for a sprint-distance tri in Bournemouth, which included an open-water ocean swim. I figured that, since we were about to have a baby, I would probably spend a lot less time going out and a lot more time being awake early in the morning. That meant less time partying, so taking up a new hobby was positive. The other catalyst for finally learning to swim properly was that Tania and I had to move to a larger flat because our old flat in Old Street, although super cool, was too small. Moving meant that we also moved to a new gym, which had a pool. It was a good opportunity to learn the front crawl, and signing up for a race gave me the motivation to do so. The only problem was that I didn't know how to go about learning.

I looked at getting swimming lessons but was put off by my experience as a teenager, and the cost of one-on-one lessons. I turned to Google, and as always the Internet had all the answers. I came across a book called *Total Immersion* by Terry Laughlin, and it became my swimming bible. I would recommend it to anyone who wants to learn how to swim the front crawl or improve their freestyle technique. It broke the task down into fourteen lessons, and by the end, I could do a comfortable front crawl. The first lesson even started with swimming on my back, which was right up my alley. The author's philosophy was that if I felt I was struggling, I was doing it wrong, and if it seemed relaxed and easy, I was doing it right. To this day, I follow this advice, and I always aim to be completely calm and comfortable in the water. The book resonated with me a lot, and it started my swimming journey. A lot of people tell me that I must be a good swimmer, but I don't think so. Swimming is so technical that I'm not even close to mastering it. I had progressed enough to attempt swimming 3.8 kilometres for an Ironman, but after all these years I still see myself as a beginner with a lot more to learn. Thankfully, I enjoy the process of learning, and swimming will be a lifelong journey to mastery for me.

I used to tell people when I started doing triathlons that I couldn't swim and had taught myself. Tania would always correct me and tell them that I was a good swimmer; I just didn't know how to do the front crawl. Technically she was right, but it was more dramatic and impressive to claim I'd taught myself using a book. (That also allows for some jokes about how to avoid getting the pages wet in the pool.) Now, I tell people that I started doing triathlons to learn how to swim, eager to motivate them to have a go themselves. It's fascinating to look back and think that when I first started I couldn't even swim a length of a pool using front crawl, and now I'm going to attempt the longest distance in the sport. This thought entered my head this morning, midway through my swim, and a huge smile crept across my face underwater. Such a journey.

Thursday, 11 May 2017

I wasted a lot of today trying to get my phone fixed. During the wedding festivities, the after-party was in our villa, and most of the guests (including myself) ended up jumping in the pool. Most were in their suits and dresses, but I was sensible and stripped down to my boxers. Then I put on a bathrobe and convinced everyone to jump in the Jacuzzi to warm up. Since it was our villa, I felt obligated to play the host and therefore had to supply the music. So I drunkenly pulled out my phone to play some tunes, and it ended up at the bottom of the tub. I have my old phone as a spare, but I need to get my current one fixed to download the data on it. It should be fixed by tomorrow, and my life back to normal.

I did manage to sneak in a run today, although it was a struggle. I don't know what happened to my running fitness. I was supposed to do an hour and forty minutes, but I had to stop twenty minutes early because I was exhausted. Even though I kept the pace quite slow, I couldn't settle into the run. The only reason I could think of is that I didn't eat before running due to my busy morning, so I'm blaming the poor run on bad nutrition.

We're currently dog-sitting my in-laws' dog Rambo for the next two weeks, and walking him contributed to my busy day. I also had a lot of things to get through for work. Plus, I had to sign off the garage, since the builders finally finished it. It only took them eleven bloody weeks! But that's not the end of it; now we have to get furniture for the spare room that we've built in the garage, because that's where we're planning on putting my parents when they visit in two weeks' time. We're glad that they're flying in from Canada to look after Sofia and Elisa while we're climbing Kilimanjaro.

Speaking of Kilimanjaro, Tania and I are starting to panic. We still need to buy a lot of stuff for the trip. The equipment list is pretty long and costly, and we have to buy two of everything, so the cost is piling up. We'd bought bits and pieces right after Christmas, but held off buying some of the expensive gear because we were budgeting for the garage, so I'm glad that's finished and we can concentrate on preparing for Kilimanjaro. Today, I bought another sleeping bag, a duffel bag, head torches and some merino-wool socks. Plus, I had to research travel insurance, which took some time because I had to ascertain that the insurance covers hiking trips up to six thousand metres.

Six thousand metres sounds daunting. Last year Tania and I hiked Ben Nevis with Caroline and another friend, to see whether we still wanted to climb Kilimanjaro afterwards. Ben Nevis is the highest peak in the British Isles at 1,345 metres. Kilimanjaro is 5,895 metres, so significantly higher. It took us about seven hours and forty-eight minutes to climb Ben Nevis and get back down. Afterwards, we were completely knackered. The following day we could barely walk, and couldn't picture ourselves going out climbing again, never mind continuing for another six days. But even though climbing Kilimanjaro seemed impossible the day after Ben Nevis, both Tania and I loved the climbing experience and knew that we wanted to give Kilimanjaro a shot. Climbing Ben Nevis gave us a taste of what it would be like, and we knew it wouldn't be easy, but we're both up for the challenge. We have about three weeks to go, and we still have a lot of things to do. But I mustn't panic; I have to focus on one thing at a time, and we'll get there eventually… hopefully.

Sunday, 14 May 2017

It has been a good weekend of training. Yesterday was full-on, and I was looking forward to the training session. As planned, I got up around 6am and got on with my routine of getting ready for a bike ride. I had a hearty breakfast and got all the nutrition ready for my ride: three gels and two energy bars, which was all I had left in the cupboard and I had doubts whether it would be enough. It was going to be a long ride, so I wasn't planning on pushing it too hard. I figured that I would eat something every forty minutes or so.

    Before starting out, I had to consider how to dress for the ride since I'd be out for about five hours. The hourly forecast was about 8°C at 7am to about 14°C around noon; quite a range. Plus, when I looked out of the window, it was raining, so I put on several layers and took waterproofs. It was the right decision as the sun only peeked through the clouds a few times. For most of the ride, it was cloudy, and the wind picked up towards the end, so I stayed warm without getting too hot.

    The next challenge was figuring out what route to do, and I decided that I would ride to Richmond Park and do four or five anticlockwise loops. Richmond Park is about 11.5 kilometres around, and there are three hills: Dark Hill, Broomfield Hill and Sawyer's Hill. The park offers two distinct routes depending on the direction you take. I would normally do a combination of clockwise and anticlockwise loops, but yesterday I decided to go only anticlockwise because it was slightly easier due to the climbs not being so steep. The Outlaw bike course is relatively flat with only a couple of climbs in the middle, so I figured I should pick a route that would match that more closely. However, I couldn't just go round and round Richmond Park as my legs would burn out from all the climbing, so I tacked on a few laps of Regent's Park at the end to get my four-and-a-half hours of riding. It worked out pretty much according to plan: I did four laps around Richmond Park and then rode to Regent's Park and did another three laps. I was disappointed when I finished and looked at my bike computer and read 98.5 kilometres. It would've been satisfying to hit a (metric) century.

I took it relatively easy, and it was annoying getting passed by a lot of people. But I'm used to getting overtaken by the hardcore cyclists that frequent Richmond Park. I even got lapped by a cycling club, which was humbling and demoralising. I consoled myself by remembering that I still had a run to do afterwards, and that I was training for an Ironman and not a sportive. Initially, it seemed that four-and-a-half hours on the road would feel long, but since I broke down the route into laps, it was easier to convince my brain to keep going. I don't mind riding loops around a park, which some people don't like. The other advantage of Richmond Park is that there are no red lights to worry about, so I could go round and round without stopping. I did, however, stop just before leaving the park for a pee break and to fill up my water bottle before heading towards Regent's Park. The only downside of riding for so long on a Saturday morning was that there was a lot of traffic by the time I exited the park. Hence, it was a lot slower getting to Regent's Park than on a normal Sunday morning.

After three short laps around Regent's Park, it was back home, and I was looking forward to getting out of the saddle. I was getting tired physically, and I had doubts about the run. But again, I just told myself to at least give it a go and see how my legs react. After a quick change into my running gear, I was out the door again to start my half-hour run. Curiously, my legs were fine, and although I purposely went at a slower pace, I had good posture and could sustain a relaxed pace. It was encouraging, and I felt fantastic afterwards.

Yesterday was a solid session, and thinking back, I cycled more than half of the bike leg of an Ironman. Afterwards, I had some energy left to do some work on the garage; I put stuff away and drilled some holes in the wall. The best part of the day was that we were invited to a kid's birthday party at Wembley Stadium to watch the women's FA Cup Final. Most children's parties are typical bouncy-castle affairs that I normally attempt to avoid, but going to Wembley for a Cup Final was unique and the kids loved it. I thought that this could only happen in London. It was a memorable experience, and it was lovely spending time with the girls. I explained the rules of football to Sofia, and I even thought about getting Elisa to try football one day. I read an article once about a family who had something like fifteen children, and one of the rules the parents had was that the kids must do a sport until they reached eighteen. I like that rule, and I will encourage Sofia and Elisa to keep active and play a sport all their lives.

After yesterday's long session, today's workout was an easy two-hour ride. The hardest part was getting out of bed this morning as I was terribly exhausted. Eventually I managed it and got going. The only problem came at the beginning of the ride as I couldn't sit down due to my sore ass. The muscles around the sit bones were still raw from yesterday, and I couldn't put any power down because it hurt. So I took it easy, which was the whole point of the session as it was meant to be a recovery ride. Eventually, the pain went away, and I went around the park at an easy pace. The recovery worked, and by the end, I felt much better. I enjoyed the rest of my Sunday with the family, and worked on tidying up the garage. Tomorrow is supposed to be a rest day or an optional recovery swim. I'll attempt swimming because it'll fit in with my schedule better. My only concern is that, if I don't take a day off, I might run down my body completely. So I guess I'll have to wait and see how I feel tomorrow morning.

Tuesday, 16 May 2017

I woke up yesterday and wanted to go for a swim, but I was exhausted. I tried to convince myself to give it a go, but since it was an optional recovery swim, I decided it would be better to take the day off and rest my body. Then last night I went to bed relatively early, and slept for over nine hours! It was unexpected considering it was a weekday. But even though I got plenty of sleep, I was still knackered, and I struggled to get going. Eventually, I managed to get out of bed and do the normal morning routine of getting the girls dressed for school and getting breakfast ready. I then headed straight to the gym after dropping them off to start my first workout of the day.

I was supposed to do a steady one-hour swim, which I thought would be easy since I've been rested, but it wasn't the case. When I got in the pool the water felt like a hot bath. It was weird swimming in such warm temperatures; almost suffocating. After the first couple of laps, I was drained. My legs and arms were extremely heavy, and I was breathing hard due to the warm water. I'd taken a bottle of water with me, and had to pour some over my head to cool down. It must've been a pretty strange sight, but I was sweating, and it was boiling. Also, my right ring finger started bothering me again. I got some pains the last time I was at the pool because I'm double-jointed, and each time my right hand entered the water, the finger bent the wrong way. After countless strokes, it must've strained the joint, and it started hurting. Consequently,

I remedied the situation by taping my middle and ring fingers together. That changed my stroke a bit, but at least there was no more pain at the beginning. But my cheap solution didn't last long, because halfway through the session the tape came off and the finger started hurting again. I had to consciously change how my hand entered the water and make sure I bent my fingers as opposed to keeping them straight. It was a huge distraction, and very annoying. I bought some real sports tape tonight, and it should do the trick next time I go swimming.

Despite all the issues in the pool, I still completed the workout, and swam 2.25 kilometres in about fifty-two minutes. I had to slow down a lot, but in the end I managed to overcome the minor problems and was glad to finish it. I guess it's beneficial to encounter these issues now, so I know I can deal with them should they arise in a race situation. Although I highly doubt that the temperature of the lake we're swimming in at Nottingham will ever reach 28°C, it was useful to know that I can at least cope with it.

According to the training plan, I was meant to do a forty-five-minute ride on the turbo trainer after my swim. But when I got home, I had a lot of work waiting for me. I thought I could squeeze in the workout, but I didn't get a chance. However, I was determined to get as much cycling done as possible as I'm way behind on my bike mileage. So, as soon as we got back from Sofia's gymnastics class this evening, I got the turbo out and set up the bike. I figured I could at least do thirty minutes while I had dinner cooking in the oven. I was pretty proud of myself for doing two workouts today. It goes to show how much time and dedication is needed for an Ironman. Balancing training with work, family and everything else is a challenge in itself. So far, I'm barely coping; not to mention I've also got Kilimanjaro to prepare for. Tania is pretty busy with work as well, and she's stressed out, but we're working together to get stuff ready, so I'm sure we'll be all right.

Thursday, 18 May 2017

Each day seems to blend into the next. Wake up, get the kids ready, drop them off at school, train, work, pick up the kids, make dinner, do some more work, sleep, repeat. The only difference seems to be the type of training I'm doing on any particular day. Yesterday it was a key running session, and I had to run for an hour and fifty minutes. During the marathon training, I did my long runs at the weekends, but for the Ironman, weekends are reserved for crazy long bike sessions with just a tiny bit of running after many hours in the saddle. Now I have to do the long runs on Wednesdays, which is trickier to fit into my schedule. Thankfully, I managed to do the run yesterday, although my pace was sluggish at about 6:09/km for about 17.5 kilometres. However, it didn't seem like I was running slower because the effort felt similar to my other long runs. So I'm uncertain why my pace had dropped. The only explanation I could think of is that my body hasn't fully recovered from the huge session at the weekend and is still adjusting to the extra workload. I'm not too worried about the pace as my main goal is to get around the Ironman course; I'm not shooting for a particular time. Well, that's a small lie, since I'm secretly aiming between fourteen and fifteen hours. However, this goal is not set in stone, and I won't be too gutted if I don't finish within that time, as long as I finish.

Perhaps part of the reason for my running slower yesterday was that I knew I couldn't completely kill my legs due to the long swim scheduled for today. Last week, I found out that the pool at my gym was not available on Thursdays due to an aquarobics class, so I switched my Wednesday long run with the Thursday long swim. Switching these two sessions is not ideal, and following the plan made more sense. Last night I came up with a solution: I will go to the community pool that is relatively close to my house. This pool is twenty-five metres long, rather than 18.2 metres like my gym pool. This would be better for simulating an open-water swim since I wouldn't be turning around as often and therefore wouldn't get the benefit of pushing off the wall. At the community pool today I swam close to an hour-and-a-half, with a total of 3,500 metres. As expected, my pace was a lot slower, but I don't know if it was because I slowed down on purpose since I knew it was a long swim, or if it was due to my tired legs from the run yesterday. Maybe it was a little of both, but the main thing was I did the swim. Plus, now I can do my long swims on Thursdays, and I don't have to switch the schedule.

I'm glad that I pushed myself and completed today's training, even though I was knackered. Swimming up and down seventy times can be daunting, and it took a lot of mental stamina to complete the workout. But I used my usual technique of breaking the session down into smaller chunks, and did my best to not think about how many laps I had to do. Instead, I focused on all the minor things that made up my swimming technique, like head position, pointing my toes, my pull and my stroke rate. I also spent a lot of time visualising different race scenarios. Before I knew it, I had done an hour-and-a-half in the pool, and I wasn't completely shattered.

While swimming I thought a lot about our upcoming Kilimanjaro trip. There are only two weeks to go, and we still have a lot of small items to purchase. We are keeping on top of it, though, so it wasn't complete panic mode yet. Tania was in charge of getting all the medical stuff, and she has a whole pharmacy's worth of drugs to take with us – malaria pills, pills for altitude sickness, antibiotics, diarrhoea pills, etc. Normally, I think she goes overboard with medicine, but in this situation, it's useful that she's a bit of a hypochondriac. It's better if we have it and don't need it, rather than need it and not have it. At over five thousand metres up on the mountain, I don't think there will be a pharmacy nearby. While Tania was busy figuring out all the medicine and first-aid kit, I ordered myself a new pair of shoes to take with me. I ordered them from Amazon, and luckily they fit perfectly. I've never ordered shoes from Amazon before, for obvious reasons such as not being able to try them on. But since I don't have time to go shopping for shoes, I thought I'd risk it, and I'm glad it worked out.

Along with the shoes came Tania's Peebol. I don't know how it works, but I think this is part of a contraption that will allow Tania to pee standing up. Obviously, this comes naturally to me, but apparently is a major issue for girls. We did some research and concluded that the Shewee-and-Peebol combo is probably the most suitable for her. Unfortunately, we didn't get a chance to test out the Shewee on one of our date hikes; we'll have to wait to see if it works.

Even though we're still too busy to get properly excited, a big part of me is looking forward to the trip. The excitement is growing, and soon enough we will be on that plane. At the same time, the parent in me is worried about leaving the girls for a whole week. It's something I need to manage, and I know that Tania and I should be strong enough to cope. There is an old Kili saying that goes, 'your attitude determines your altitude'. I smiled as I read this tonight. Our adventure looms…

Sunday, 21 May 2017

Last week I enjoyed the Sunday recovery ride after the hard Saturday session, and I was looking forward to today's being the same. The weather looked lovely, and I was out the door by about 7.15am. Oddly, my legs felt rather good considering the long day yesterday. However, as soon as I got to Regent's Park, it was windy, and it didn't take long before I started getting tired from pushing against it. Since drafting behind another cyclist is not allowed during the triathlon, I just let other riders pass me instead of slipstreaming behind them. However, after a while, I realised that, I was exerting a lot of effort riding on my own against the wind, and it would be better if I just drafted behind a group. I was about halfway through my two-hour ride, and as a group passed me, I tried to hang on their wheels. It turned out I could hang on for a long time. When a faster group went past, I decided to switch and latched on to them instead, to see how I would fare. Again, I was surprised at how my legs woke up, and I kept up with them. I revel riding in a peloton, especially when the pace was just right and I could stick with the group without working too hard.

The peloton took some getting used to, and I'm sure that I still have a lot to learn. For one thing, I was a complete 'wheel suck', meaning that I stayed at the back and didn't take any turns up front. It is akin to being a greedy bastard who always takes and gives nothing in return. However, in my defence, I reckoned that I wasn't fast enough to pull up front; plus I didn't know how to rotate myself to lead the pack. There were a few rare occasions when someone drafted behind me and I let them, simply because I didn't know how to let them pass so that they could take a turn up front. In any case, it was exhilarating riding in a fast group. The long ride the previous week must have helped improve my form. Hopefully, over the next few weeks, I can continue keeping pace with the fast bunch.

It was such a thrill riding in the group that I didn't want to go home, but I had a busy Sunday full of DIY plans so I had to stick to the schedule. In the end, my recovery ride was two hours and five minutes, and I rode for about fifty-one kilometres. When I checked my stats on Strava I saw a little gold medal icon indicating a new personal best for one lap around Regent's Park. I'd managed to ride the five-kilometre loop in eight minutes and ten seconds, which was about two minutes faster than my average time. Not bad for a recovery ride. Now I'm looking forward to the coming weeks to see how much more I'll improve.

Tuesday, 23 May 2017

Terrible news to wake up to. At a concert in Manchester last night, a suicide bomber killed twenty-two people and injured hundreds more. There were children amongst the dead; one girl only eight years old. As a parent, I can't help but go through the what-if scenarios, and I can't even begin to imagine what it must be like for the parents of the children who died. Tania and I have got Sofia concert tickets for her birthday, and I'm slightly anxious about the event. However, I have to reason with myself: this is exactly what the terrorists want, and if we allow ourselves to be cowed then they win. Therefore, to stand up against this hideous act, we must show defiance and continue with our daily lives. One day, I wish that each of us can understand each other more and perhaps eventually realise that we're all one human race and what many perceive as religious or racial divides don't exist. A lot of these thoughts occupied my head while I was swimming today.

The thermostat at the pool gym is still broken, and the water was really warm. At times, it felt warmer than bathwater and made for an uncomfortable swim; bordering on hot, and it was almost claustrophobic being submerged in it. It brought back memories of the first swim race I did, back in 2010 when I entered my first mile-long open-water event. I entered it to gain experience in swimming longer distances in preparation for an Olympic-distance triathlon the following year. At the time, the farthest I'd swum was eight hundred metres during a sprint-distance triathlon. I still considered myself a slow newbie. Swimming a mile in open water was a major challenge. It was a sunny day, and at first the swim went off okay. As usual, after a couple of hundred metres, I was dropped by the pack and was swimming near the back with the stragglers. But even though I was slow, I was comfortable enough, and the pace was sustainable. I remembered thinking that this wasn't too bad, and that I could make it. But then we swam under a bridge, and a huge shadow was cast over us. I don't know why it triggered it, but I started panicking due to the sudden darkness. My breaths became shorter, and for no reason at all, I was struggling to breathe. I was claustrophobic, and it felt like the dark water was pulling me down. The panic started to consume me, and every time I tried to breathe, I just kept swallowing water. Then, just when I thought that I might drown, I focused on something else. I closed my eyes and started thinking about Sofia. That calmed me down immediately, and I pictured her as this enormous, warm, bright light under the water, rising from deep below to lift me up and keep me afloat. That thought was so powerful and so soothing that I was able to calmly turn my head and take a wonderful breath of fresh air. All of a sudden, I passed from under the shadow of the bridge and was back in the beautiful warm sunshine.

I don't know how long that whole episode lasted for, but it seemed like ages. I learned an important lesson then, about how powerful our thoughts can be and how thinking about my family can easily lift me up. When I exited the water, I knew that I'd fought for my smile that day.

Sofia was still a toddler at that time. From the first time I held her and Elisa in my arms, they have given us so much joy. I've enjoyed every minute of being a dad to both of them; it's my biggest challenge and my greatest achievement. These thoughts swirled through my head during my swim today, and every time I took a breath I had a little grin.

Friday, 26 May 2017

The past few days have been quite manic. I had a problem with one of the servers at work that kept me tied up on Tuesday and

Wednesday. Despite this, I still managed to sneak a one-hour run during lunch, even though I was pretty tired from working late the night before. I needed a run for some stress relief and to be re-energised after working flat out. It also helped me deal with the server problem by going over possible solutions in my head. After fixing the server on Wednesday, I went out to do a pub quiz with a few of the local dads. It turned out to be a fantastic evening as we ended up winning, plus we also won the bonus round, and shared the £350 prize between the five of us. But the best part was the team name we used – 'And in First Place' – which was meant to confuse the quizmaster as we were sure we'd never come in first. As it turned out, it became a self-fulfilling prophecy. It was brilliant, and the bartender commented that he'd never seen any team win so triumphantly.

 The only downside was that I drank too much and I got home late. Consequently, it was another night of little sleep. I spent yesterday morning driving to the airport to pick up my parents. The traffic was horrendous, and my tiredness compounded it. To top it off, I punctured a tyre just after I dropped off Elisa at nursery, so I was extremely late by the time I got to the airport. But that didn't matter because seeing my parents was lovely, and the looks on their faces when they saw Sofia and Elisa later were priceless.

 I had to skip training yesterday and moved the swim session to today. Since the pool's thermostat at my gym is still broken, I went to the community sports centre instead. The longer pool is better for training, so I'm considering switching to it permanently. The lanes are also wider, so passing or being passed – typically the latter – was easier. I also practised sighting, which should pay dividends on race day.

 This week is supposed to be a rest week, so my workouts are shorter and easier. However, since we're leaving for Kilimanjaro next Friday, tomorrow I will do my long workout instead. I know I can do it, but Tania is laying on the guilt trip because my parents are in town and she thinks that I should spend more time with them. But we've already planned a whole week of activities, so I figured they won't mind if I go for a six-hour bike ride tomorrow.

Saturday, 27 May 2017

After sleeping on it, I decided it was probably best to keep today's ride shorter in order to keep Tania onside. I didn't want to push my luck as I know the Saturday rides will only get longer and longer. Consequently, I did four laps around Richmond Park and then a twenty-minute run. The ride still added up to about seventy-two kilometres; a significant distance. I managed to get out of the house by 7am, and bright sunshine greeted me. The park was busy with cyclists by the time I got there.

As I pedalled up Sawyer's Hill on my first loop, I was astonished that I could keep up with faster cyclists. I didn't even touch the front derailleur for an easier gear all the way up, and managed to stay on the larger cog. I smiled for a change, as opposed to grimacing up the climb. I kept the tempo high until halfway through when it started raining. Naturally, I slowed down, but I didn't pull over, unlike some cyclists who took shelter under a tree. Then when I got to the fast, steep descent down Broomfield Hill, a driver in a car going the other way was waving his hands up and down out the window, motioning for cyclists to slow down. I thought it was just because of the rain, but I soon realised there had been an accident. It had happened at the steepest bend of the descent, and a few cyclists were already on the scene helping out. I got a quick glimpse of the fallen rider, and she looked bad. The descent was so steep that I was squeezing both brakes and yet still going fast, and as soon as I let go, I picked up speed quickly. From what I gathered, the cyclist who'd come off might not be a regular rider: she was wearing trainers and a regular gym outfit as opposed to cycling shoes and Lycra. I'm not a cycling snob, but around Richmond Park you could easily tell the difference between recreational riders and regular road cyclists. Most roadies would have matching jerseys, bib shorts and socks, with some even coordinating their kit with their shoes and bike. I'm guilty myself of making sure that the kit I'm wearing at least looks the part, even though I get dropped by most people, sometimes even by unassuming recreational riders wearing baggy jeans in hybrid bikes.

As I went past the accident, it dawned on me why I'd seen at least three ambulances parked in different places around the park last week. There are so many cyclists in Richmond Park that accidents must be common. I know that crashes are part of cycling and I've had three myself since I've been riding road bikes. The first was years ago when I was training for a hundred-kilometre sportive. Back then, I had my first beginner's road bike, and I was out riding with two friends. I had never tackled such a long distance before, and I didn't have experience with nutrition. After riding for hours, we hit a short but steep climb. Due to exhaustion, I had a momentary lapse in concentration which led to me brushing against a fence and down I went. I wasn't going fast because we were climbing, so I didn't hurt myself. But disaster struck a few kilometres down the road, when my rear derailleur broke off. It was unrepairable, and I had a miserable long walk to the train station in cleats.

My second crash was during a race in Hyde Park. It was an Olympic-distance triathlon, and the course was wet and windy. There were a lot of sharp turns, and on a fast corner, the guy in front of me slid off and went down. There was no way of avoiding him, so I crashed on top of him. With adrenaline pumping, my first instinct was to make sure my bike was fine, then asked the guy that he was okay. I checked myself and noticed a nasty bruise on my leg, and some scratches. After asking the marshal who was helping us if it was okay to continue, I quickly remounted and got back to racing. I can't remember the result of that race, but I do recall telling everyone about the crash as if it was a badge of honour.

My latest crash was last year when I was coming back from Richmond Park after a training ride. While I was in the park, it had started to rain, so I had to stop and put on my rain jacket. But on the way home, it stopped raining and the sun came out, so I was getting too hot. I decided to take the jacket off and saw a perfect place to pull over. I was riding along the river, and the kerb was very low, so I could easily ride over it. I slowed down enough to mount the kerb, but I must've hit it at the wrong angle, and since it was wet my front tyre slipped off and before I knew it I was on the ground. It was a bad crash, and I remember rolling on my back and just looking at the sky struggling to work out what had happened. Then the adrenaline kicked in, and immediately I was up picking up my bike, and found a bench to sit down. I assessed the damage: my mouth was bleeding, my chin hurt, there were deep cuts on my left ring finger and I had some serious road rash on my left knee. My first concern was my mouth, and I tried to see if the bleeding was internal. Luckily, it turned out to be just a cut lip. As I was assessing my mouth, another cyclist noticed that I'd come off and immediately stopped to help. The guy was very kind and helped me compose myself and check out my bike. There wasn't too much damage apart from a slightly bent front wheel and some scrapes and scratches, so I could still ride it. The helpful Samaritan even asked other passers-by for some water and tissues to clean my wound. With his help, I eventually managed to recover enough to ride home. It was the worst crash I've had, and I was off the bike for days. My knee took the longest to heal, but fortunately it healed sufficiently before my half-Ironman two weeks later.

The thoughts of my previous crashes reminded me that cycling could be dangerous. It doesn't matter whether you're a newbie or a seasoned pro; accidents happen, and you have to be careful at all times. On my second lap around the park, the ambulance was at the scene attending to the girl who'd crashed. Then on my third lap, I saw the paramedics injecting something into her back, which I can only guess was an epidural. It looked like she was in bad shape, and I can only pray that she'll be okay.

Monday, 29 May 2017

The weekend has been busy. We've eaten out every day since my parents arrived. When I weighed myself this morning, I'd gained a kilo, despite the amount of exercise I've been doing. I wondered how this could be possible, then I realised that the tapas, the nachos, the pizza and the large picnic probably had something to do with it.

Yesterday, I did a fifty-kilometre recovery ride around Regent's Park. I was supposed to ride slowly, but right from the start, I wanted to test my legs and see if I could keep up with some of the faster guys. I reckoned that my legs were getting stronger and, since Regent's Park is flat, it should be possible to stay tucked behind a group. After a few warm-up laps, a peloton riding at a steady clip went past, and I latched on the back. The pace was faster than I could do on my own, but since I was drafting behind, the effort seemed considerably less. I was grinning the whole way around, happily hanging on the wheel of the faster guys.

After the weekend's easier workload, today's swim would be a breeze. However, the pool thermostat at the gym is still broken, and the water was even hotter than last week. It was uncomfortable, and I desperately wanted to stop, but I thought it would be a good opportunity to build my mental toughness. I know that there would be times during the race when I would want to quit, so I pretended that this was one of those times and figured out a way of overcoming it. I couldn't bear the heat, and

I was actually sweating. It was bizarre; as if I was swimming in a steam room. To get through the ordeal, I concentrated on my breathing. For most of the swim, all I focused on was breathing slowly and being as relaxed as possible. It seemed to work, and eventually I forgot about the heat and got into a rhythm. Before I knew it, I'd swum a mile and finished the workout. I couldn't wait to get out of the pool and cool down under a cold shower. But before doing so, I made a note not to go back to that pool again.

Kilimanjaro is less than a week away, and we're struggling not to panic! Over the weekend we attempted to pack, but we didn't have much luck. We ended up making a big mess in our room, and just shoved everything into our duffel bags. It was hard work, especially with two energetic girls jumping around wanting to help, and just being a hindrance. We did manage to do our last-minute shopping, and we've ticked off everything on the long list of stuff we needed to get. We must've spent a small fortune by now. Hopefully, we'll use most of the stuff more than once and do other expeditions in the future.

I checked out the weather for Kilimanjaro and was concerned to see that the forecast is for rain and snow every day. June to October is supposed to be one of the best periods to climb the mountain, but the rainy season usually lasts until May and sometimes mid-June. Now it's looking like it'll be wet and cold when we climb it. Obviously not ideal, but at least we'll get to use all the rain and cold-weather gear we've bought.

Today we had to organise all the things my parents might need while we're away. This included planning for the worst, which meant writing our wills. I know it sounds morbid, but Tania and I are practical people, and we owe it to our daughters to ensure that they are taken care of should anything happen to either of us. Writing a will was difficult, and I can't help worrying about the girls while we are away. However, we have some peace of mind knowing that our trekking company will be sending daily update emails to my parents while we are on the mountain. Also, Tania read that there might be mobile coverage pretty much all the way to the summit, with just a few black spots along the way. For that reason, she bought a spare power bank to charge our phones, and the plan is to keep both phones off and only turn them on to make quick calls to the girls. Touch wood we can at least speak to them each day.

Even though there are still a lot of things to organise, I am starting to feel excited about the trip. In the meantime, I have plenty of work to finish to keep me occupied, and the relentless Ironman training to think of.

Wednesday, 31 May 2017

We're relieved that we finally got most of our packing done today. We still have a few things to do over the next two days, but so far we're on top of things. Work-wise, I have a couple of things that I want to finish tomorrow, and then I can finally start getting fully excited for the trip. Elisa is settling in warmly with my parents, which put us at ease. We were worried that my parents would find it hard to look after her, but so far it's going pretty well. Of course, the girls will always be on our minds, but at least we know that they're in safe hands.

When I woke up today, I wasn't expecting a long workout, so my heart sank when I checked the training schedule and found that I had to run twenty-five kilometres. I wasn't prepared for it, plus I've been going to bed quite late over the past few nights after chatting to my parents. Consequently, it was a real struggle to get going this morning, and I wasn't sure whether I could actually run twenty-five kilometres, considering that I did a two-kilometre swim yesterday, plus an hour on the turbo trainer afterwards. I was knackered, and it took a while to convince myself to get my ass out the door. As I expected, the first three kilometres were a slog even though I was going slow. My brain was telling me that there was no way I could run over half a marathon's distance. But I told it to shut up, changed my focus and broke down the run into shorter segments. This made my mind cooperate and start thinking more positively and I started enjoying the run. Despite being drained, I eventually finished it. I stopped many times, and my overall pace was 6:02/km; quite a way off from when I was training for the marathon. But I'm not too concerned because I know that when I start the running leg of the Ironman, my pace will probably be a lot slower. For me, the Ironman is not about going fast, but simply being able to finish it. There is also a good chance that I will be walking a lot of the time. I'm already planning on breaking up the run into five-kilometre chunks, with some walking mixed in. Therefore, most of my run training will be at a slow pace in order to save my legs for the rest of the training week. Tomorrow, I have to do a 3.5-kilometre swim, and it'll be interesting to see how my legs feel after today's long run.

 My friend Colette texted me today to wish us luck for the climb. It's nice to know that there are a lot of people out there thinking about our upcoming adventure. Colette was one of my flatmates when I first moved to London. We lived in a shared house which we all referred to as '158' because of the house number. (Not overly creative, but apt.) The house had six bedrooms: five doubles and one single. Officially there were only supposed to be eleven people living there and paying rent. Unofficially there were at least fifteen to nineteen staying in the house on any given night. It was like living in a hostel with different languages spoken from several countries. We had Kiwis, Aussies, Saffas, Brazilians, Frenchies, Polish, sometimes English and a Canuck (me). We were all relatively young, always wanting to travel, but always skint; living it up in London, working to save enough money to fund our next trip. The best thing about 158 was that, when I got home every night, there were always interesting people to hang out with. More often than not, there'd be a small party in the lounge due to the constant stream of dossers staying over. We all had friends who were passing through London and needed a place to stay. I would come home to a lounge full of people having a glass of wine and a couple of spliffs. It was a special time, and I formed some incredible friendships. Colette was one of those, and we managed 158 together.

Coincidentally, Colette is also planning a trip to Kilimanjaro this year. We tried to arrange to do the climb together, but we couldn't make it happen. She has booked her trip for August, so we will be walking a similar path, albeit at different times.

I was living in 158 when I first met Tania back in September 2003. I met her on my twenty-sixth birthday when Caroline took me clubbing in London. We went to a drum 'n' bass night at Fabric, which was my first proper clubbing experience in London. Fabric is a famous club with three massive spaces hosting resident and guest DJs playing drum 'n' bass, dubstep, house and techno. We had pre-drinks at a pub beforehand, and that was where I met Tania. She went to university with Caroline, and came out to say hello along with her friend. They didn't plan to go to Fabric and didn't have tickets for the club, but after a couple of drinks, she decided that she wanted to go for a bit of a dance. I, on the other hand, slowly got drunk. I was nervous because I knew I'd be dropping a pill that night. I thought Tania was pretty cool for going to Fabric on a whim, and she just stayed for a few hours without taking anything. But not me; I dropped the pill and the next thing I knew I was on the side stage in Fabric's main room. As the pill started to work, there was a period where I lost all sense of time. Then I came around, and for some reason, I couldn't remember my name. Then I looked down and thought, *why am I standing by the ocean?* before realising that what I'd thought was water was actually the dance floor full of bobbing heads. Eventually, my brain focused, and I remembered who and where I was. Then I felt the heavy bass pounding hard against my chest. The music took control, and I danced for hours with the DJ in full command of my body. It was a fantastic birthday, and I didn't even know just then that I had just met my future wife.

Thursday, 01 June 2017

I reached my fundraising goal! Last night I posted an update to my JustGiving page to let everyone know that Tania and I will soon be off to Kilimanjaro. I promised everyone who donated that I will dedicate part of the climb to them. It pushed me over the threshold, and so far I have raised £1,029 for Cancer Research UK. This gives me a real boost for the upcoming challenge.

Despite the long run yesterday, I still swam 3.1 kilometres today. I thought it would be impossible to even get out of bed, considering that yesterday I ran a half-marathon distance. But training has become automatic and routine for me, and now my body seeks it. I feel guilty if I miss a session, and I plan every day around my training. This week, I have my parents helping with the girls, so it has been easier to schedule. I was able to leave the house at six this morning to get my swim out of the way. I went to the bigger pool, which I think is better for me. However, I was disappointed that my pace has dropped significantly; I was about ten to fifteen seconds slower per hundred metres, which was disheartening. Perhaps I was slower because I couldn't push off the walls as much. But there are a lot of positives with training in the longer pool, so I will stick with it.

The larger pool also allowed me to practise sighting, which I could use. Sometimes I still swim crookedly even with the lane markers at the bottom of the pool to guide me; and there's nothing more painful and annoying than getting tangled in the pool-lane buoys. The other positive about the bigger pool is that the lanes are wider and busier. Most people would find that annoying, but I see it as useful practice for a race. The start of the swim in most triathlons is manic, and it's like being in a washing machine. There are bodies everywhere, with flying elbows and kicking legs. People swimming over the top of you, and being dunked underwater, are not uncommon. It is useful to simulate this in a busy pool in order to practise staying calm in choppy waters with people swimming all around me.

It's the eve of our Kilimanjaro trip, and I wonder what sort of choppy waters we will encounter there. We just need to make sure that we stay calm and positive through it all.

As I drove home, I reflected upon when I started seeing Tania. After Fabric, I didn't see her again until a couple of months later, during a Halloween party at 158. I invited Caroline, who in turn invited Tania. However, there was a miscommunication between them and Tania ended up coming without Caroline, but with her boyfriend, her younger brother and his girlfriend. That was the first time I realised that Tania had a boyfriend and they were living together. After finding this out, I automatically thought of her as off-limits and nothing more than a friend. By that time, I'd learned a few things about women, including that it was better to just try to get to know them as friends, even if I was attracted to them. I learned to get past my attraction and genuinely strive to get to know a woman, not because I want to get into her pants, but because I find it friendlier to get to know people so that I can hang out with them. When I learned that Tania was living with someone, I thought that that was cool. I would aim to get to know her as a friend, because even though I found her very attractive, she was off-limits. I wasn't the homewrecker type.

After Halloween, Tania and I arranged to meet up and hang out again. We went for coffee once, even though I don't drink coffee. Then, just before Christmas, we decided to check out Portobello Market in Notting Hill. As we were shopping, my hands brushed up against hers and we ended up just naturally holding hands. At the time, I thought perhaps it was normal for two friends to hold hands in England. Little did I know that our friendship was slowly mutating into something much more. But she was still living with her boyfriend, so I didn't think anything of it.

For Christmas that year, I decided to go to Andorra by myself and spend the holidays snowboarding. Before I left, I briefly met up with Tania again to exchange Christmas cards. Again, it was platonic, and in the card I wrote that hopefully the following year we could go skiing together, which was funny because the following year we did end up going skiing together! But at the time, I just thought of her as a friend I liked hanging out with.

After Christmas, I was assigned to work at MTV in London. Originally I'd been working in Windsor and had a long commute, so it was terrific to work in London, and going out for drinks afterwards was a lot easier. I met up with Caroline and Tania in Leicester Square. That night, my knee touched Tania's, and that was when I realised that there might be something more to our friendship. Perhaps it was the booze, but I started to think of her as more than a friend. But again, to me she was off-limits, and I was happy enough to just hang out with her. It got messy that evening. She got really drunk and ended up puking on the Tube. She was in such a state that I decided to get off at her stop and catch the bus home with her to make sure she got there okay. After dropping her off, I didn't know where the hell I was. This was before smartphones, so I called my friend Slater in Canada and asked him to look up a map on his computer and direct me home. I told him that I got lost after walking home a really cool girl.

Leicester Square was the start of our regular nights out. Soon afterwards, Tania, Caroline and I started meeting up for drinks frequently after work. But after a while, for one reason or another Caroline couldn't show up, and it ended up with just Tania and me. During one of those nights, I told Tania that

Caroline had mentioned to me that she felt uneasy around her because she didn't like her boyfriend. It turned out that Tania's boyfriend had made a pass on Caroline before, and she'd disliked him ever since. That same night, Tania confided in me that she had been sleeping on the couch and had been wanting to break up with her boyfriend. She just didn't know how, because she felt like his mum as opposed to his girlfriend. She'd feel bad if she broke up with him because he was from Italy and didn't have many friends in London.

There were a lot of revelations that night, and at the end of the evening, we kissed for the first time. It wasn't intentional; it just happened. But we were both drunk, and I felt bad the following day, so we decided not to meet up again until she sorted out her situation with her boyfriend.

We didn't see each other for two weeks, but we still sent emails and chatted online. Colette thought that Tania was in a difficult situation and that the break-up wouldn't be easy, especially since they were living together. But Tania surprised me when she managed to do it. She broke up with him, gave up their flat and he moved back to Italy. Tania ended up moving into my tiny room in 158, and we've been together ever since. It was lovely, and we would always wake up with warm smiles on our faces. It's more than thirteen years since we embarked on our journey together. We have shared so many incredible experiences since then, and tomorrow we're off on another adventure!

Saturday, 03 June 2017

Flying without the girls was a real treat for us. We were able to wander leisurely around the airport without having to look up every two seconds checking on them. We had time to browse the shops and talk without having to be in parent mode. The flight was like a holiday in itself. We flew with Qatar Airways, and the service was way better than with the budget airlines we usually use.

Other than the luxury of travelling without kids, the flight was uneventful. We had a layover in Doha where we learned that it is illegal to eat in public spaces during daylight hours in the holy month of Ramadan. We were confused because we weren't sure if the airport was considered a public space. Most of the restaurants were closed, so we erred on the side of caution and decided to wait until we boarded our next flight. To pass the time, we tried to work out which passengers were going to be climbing Kilimanjaro like us. They were easy to spot based on their daypacks or – the dead giveaway – clunky hiking boots. Some guidebooks recommended wearing your hiking boots on the plane in case the airline misplaced your luggage. Clearly, a lot of people were following that advice, whereas Tania and I just gambled on Qatar Airways not losing ours. It wasn't an issue anyway when we got to Kilimanjaro International Airport.

The airport was tiny, and it was chaotic filling out the landing paperwork and paying for our entry visas. But there were no dramas, and we got through security without any problems. Our tour operator is called Climb Kili, and their driver was waiting for us when we stepped out of the airport. Soon we were on our way to the hotel. My first impressions of Tanzania was that it was quaint. The rural scenery reminded me of the Philippines and Thailand. Our driver, Simon, seemed genuinely friendly, and merrily chatted with us all the way to the hotel. The traffic was horrible, and there was only one road to Arusha from the airport. There didn't seem to be any rhyme or reason to how people drove; cars would suddenly pull into the wrong lane, which was scary.

We passed a dodgy-looking neighbourhood just before the hotel; that put me on alert, but once we got inside the hotel compound, I was able to relax. Still, I don't see us wandering around outside the hotel gates by ourselves any time soon. We don't have time anyway, since we have one night here in the hotel and then tomorrow we start our climb. After we arrived, we walked to the hotel garden and met our guide, Herment, who seems good-natured. He gave us a quick brief and informed us that there would be six other people climbing with us. We were delighted because we thought that it would be just the two of us. We're excited to meet the others.

After meeting Herment, we relaxed in our room and then headed to the hotel restaurant for an early dinner. It was quiet: just Tania and me, plus another girl eating on her own. I looked over wondering if she'd be climbing with us and asked Tania if we should say hello. But we were pretty tired, so we decided to just find out tomorrow. With only three of us in the restaurant, I thought the food would arrive quickly; however, it took over an hour to be served. I didn't mind too much; perhaps this is just the way it is in Tanzania. After dinner, we repacked our bags and took out some stuff that we won't need for the climb. Then we called Sofia and Elisa to say hello. We thought it would be a whole week before we could speak to them again, but Herment reassured us earlier that there is a phone signal on the mountain and we could make calls throughout the week.

All we have to do now is get some sleep. I'm sure I'll be grinning in my dreams, as our adventure awaits.

Sunday, 04 June 2017

After a restless night, I was wide awake before 6am local time, which is three hours ahead of London. As much as I wanted to get some sleep, I found it difficult due to my excitement, and probably some jet lag. I didn't want to wake up Tania, so I quietly picked up my phone and browsed the BBC website, and was shocked to see a headline about another terrorist attack in London. I sat right up and continued reading, to learn that someone had driven into pedestrians on London Bridge, then gone around stabbing people. It was highly distressing news to wake up to, especially when my parents had been at the same location the week before, enjoying Borough Market. Due to the time difference, the attack had only happened about four hours ago, and the story was still developing. There were already six people confirmed dead and dozens more injured. It was awful news, and I worried about the girls and my parents back home. I knew that they were okay, but I wanted to call them again to be certain. When Tania eventually woke up, we turned on the TV and watched the news. We were both thinking about the girls and desperately wanted to say hello to them. But it was still the middle of the night in London so we couldn't call them. Eventually, we reassured ourselves that we had just spoken to them; they are fine and will be okay. So we put the terrible news aside and started our day.

After packing our bags, it was off to breakfast; we were excited to meet the people we're climbing with. It was a buffet-style continental breakfast, so we didn't have to wait hours for the food. I made sure I had more than enough to eat because I don't know what type of food we'll be served on the mountain. There weren't that many people staying at the hotel; in fact, it was just Tania and me for most of the breakfast. Then a tall guy came in wearing hiking boots, which was a dead giveaway that he's going climbing as well. After a brief introduction, we learned that his name is Rinze and he's climbing Kilimanjaro with his wife. He seems likeable and friendly, and I think he's someone we can get on with. He and his wife got in late last night, and he told us there were three Americans from their flight who checked into our hotel and will most likely be in our group too. I have met a lot of Americans while travelling. Most were nice people, but some were the stereotypical loud, obnoxious types. I'm slightly worried that these will be the latter and we'll be stuck with them for seven days.

After breakfast, we sat in the lounge and eagerly waited for everybody to show up. Soon enough, the three jet-lagged Americans walked in, and I introduced myself to Jamie, Lauren and John. I'm relieved because they don't seem like the loud, obnoxious type, although it could just be because they all looked really tired. We made small talk while we waited for the porters to sort out all the equipment and load the trucks. I didn't chat much as I knew we have seven days ahead of us to get to know each other.

Then we met Rinze's wife, Anna, who was busy sorting out her bag and doing some last-minute preparations. Finally, we met Monique, who was travelling by herself. She was (I guessed correctly) a Kiwi, but introduced herself as an Aussie because that's where she lives. So that's our Kili climbing crew, and based on first impressions, everyone seemed easy-going and friendly. I'm really glad that we're going in a group, and looking forward to getting to know all of them.

The porters eventually finished loading all the gear onto the bus, and we were finally off. The ride from Arusha to the Machame Gate was about an hour-and-a-half, but there was traffic, and we stopped several times to pick up more porters. We also stopped at a street-side butcher shop, where, I imagined, the cook bought some fresh meat for our trip. I wondered how they would keep it fresh for the next seven days. The logistics of the trip must be quite complicated. But I pushed these thoughts out of my head and just soaked in the scenery and landscape out of the bus window. I sensed huge excitement from all of us, and at the same time, a tinge of anxiety. Our group looked tired after our long flights, and I could tell that we'd all had little sleep. I attempted to get some sleep on the bus, but I was too excited. I still couldn't believe we were actually in Africa, about to embark on our adventure.

Kilimanjaro has several routes to the summit, one of which is called the Machame Route. It is also referred to as the 'Whisky

Route', given its reputation for being a tougher climb than the easier Marangu Route, which is known as the 'Coca-Cola Route'. Once we arrived at Machame Gate, there was more waiting around. The place was full of different groups getting ready to start their climbs. Our guide was busy sorting out formalities such as weighing luggage for the porters, paying park fees and sorting out our lunch. Our only task was to sign the registration book and wait. We started chatting to get to know our group, and I surveyed the climbers around me checking out their clothing and gear.

When I'm travelling, I play a game in my head while I'm people-watching. I would guess where other tourists are from based on what they are wearing, how they look or what bags they have. The second part of the game is to try and find out if I'm correct, normally by listening to them speak, either by eavesdropping or striking up a conversation. I find this game quite amusing and a fun way to pass the time. Today, it was particularly easy, as each person was carrying a lot of easily recognisable gear. For example, if someone is carrying a Kathmandu bag, there is a high chance that they're a Kiwi or an Aussie. Similarly, most Germans would have a Deuter rucksack, the Brits would be sporting Karrimor, the Canadians MEC and Osprey for the Yanks. The French, Spanish and most other Europeans will most likely have Quechua; a good and affordable brand from Decathlon, where Tania and I had bought most of our stuff. Apart from their daypacks, another giveaway was the finisher's T-shirts from various races. I counted two Ironmans, three half-Ironmans and seven marathons. I found it amusing because I know each of them was wearing their shirt like a badge of honour. It's a good way to boast about their previous achievements and show everyone how tough they are. I should know, since I've packed one half-Ironman and two marathon shirts myself, although I wasn't wearing mine yet because I don't like to brag.

Eventually, we were given our lunch, which we ate as we watched most of the other groups depart. Our lunch was disappointing compared to what the other groups were given. It consisted of plain crisps, bread and some fruit. I was slightly worried that the food was going to be the same all the way up, but I remained positive that it would get better. We had a lot of leftovers, which we gave to the monkeys that were all around us. That kept us entertained while we waited even longer, and it started to dawn on me that we would be the last group to set off.

Finally, after what seemed like forever, we began our hike. Herment introduced us to the three other guides, but the only name I retained was Anton. The other guides were still busy organising the porters, so we started off with just Anton leading us. He is a diminutive man with a friendly face. His English is not as good as Herment's, but he spoke enough to convey some facts about the flora and fauna around us. He told us that today we would be walking for about eleven kilometres and it should take about five hours. We were all eager to get going, and I heard a lot of chatter from the group at the beginning. The first few hundred metres were on paved roads, and I was slightly disappointed as I saw a lot of other groups ahead of us. I secretly hoped that it wouldn't be that busy all the way up, as I would prefer it to be quieter. My wish was soon granted as the faster groups went ahead of us, and we passed the other slower groups. We followed Anton's slow pace and were constantly reminded of *'pole, pole'*, which means 'slowly, slowly' in Swahili. This was fine as the path immediately kicked up, and suddenly we were all breathing hard. It took a while but eventually we settled into the rhythm and managed to climb at an easy conversational pace.

At the beginning, small groups started to form, and I found myself walking with Anna and Monique. We started trying to get to know each other, and I made it more entertaining by playing a game instead of asking direct questions. For example, instead of asking what we all do, I concocted a Twenty Questions game where we took turns asking questions, and the person was only allowed to answer yes or no. It made it more interesting for everyone, and it was a witty way to break the ice. Plus, we were going to be stuck with each other for the next seven days, so we had to stretch out our conversations. Through the game, we correctly guessed that Anna is in HR for a large global firm. However, we failed to guess that Monique has a law degree and is working for a law firm. Although we did mention solicitors three times, somehow we didn't guess it, probably because she didn't look like a solicitor, but to be fair she did mention that she's having second thoughts about her profession. She's in Africa partly to reassess whether she wants to continue down that path.

As we continued climbing, the temperature started to get colder and colder. It was humid, and there was a lot of moisture in the air. We were still in the jungle canopy, and we couldn't see much else apart from all the trees around us. It was like that for hours, but eventually the trees started to thin out. Then we started noticing small drops of water as the path wound its way up. Looking back down, I could see pockets of clouds, which explains the moisture and humidity in the air. The view was cool, and it got even better when there was a clear break between the trees; as we glanced up, we were treated to our first view of Kilimanjaro. The mountain loomed in the distance. It was inspiring, but at the same time the enormity of the task dawned on us.

We took plenty of breaks as nature called frequently. During one stop, Tania pulled out her Shewee peeing device and walked off behind a tree. As I watched her stroll towards me, I asked her how it went, and I laughed when she nodded with a wide smile, giving a thumbs up. She said it was a big success, and is looking forward to not having to squat down. I joked that she was now one of the boys, and said welcome to the club.

After about three hours of walking it became apparent that Jamie was struggling to keep up. We were spending more and more time stopping and waiting for her to catch up. We still only had Anton to guide us, so we had to wait as he stayed behind to walk with Jamie. But eventually, Herment and another guide, Gaston, caught up with us. By then we were all tired and eager to get to camp. The guides decided to split up the group, with me, Tania, Anna, Rinze and Lauren going ahead with Anton, while John and Monique hung back with Jamie, Herment and Gaston.

Our group pushed faster as we raced to reach camp before dark. I sighed when we eventually arrived at Machame Camp, our first campsite. Stopping the GPS tracker on my watch, I read 11.4 kilometres in five-and-a-half hours with 1,128 metres of ascent. While I waited my turn to sign the camp's registration book, I noticed that it was almost 7pm. When I stepped out of the ranger's hut after signing, I had to take out my head torch as I couldn't see anything. We were shown our tents, and then our guide told us to get ready for dinner. The porters had a washbasin set up, so we just dumped our bags in our tent, washed our hands and stepped into the dining tent. I chuckled at the two tables set up with eight chairs, warmly lit by solar-powered fairy lights and two candles. The tables were covered in a restaurant-style, red-and-black plaid tablecloth; on top there were two hot thermoses plus a large bowl of popcorn waiting. We sat down and leaned back after our long day. I saw exhausted faces, but relieved eyes. As we munched on the popcorn, we voiced our concern for the others.

Earlier, when I was researching the trip, I watched a video of a group climbing the mountain. I was amused to see that, for their lunches, their porters set up a table with a tablecloth, and it looked a lot like they were in an outdoor restaurant. It looked very civilised, and not exactly like roughing it. It's funny that we found ourselves in a similar situation. However, I'm not complaining, and welcome the small luxury.

While we waited for the others, one of the porters came in and asked us to join him outside. He led us to a tiny tent about one metre on each side, to show us how to use the toilet. The portable toilet is a cool contraption that resembles a proper toilet. It even has a hand pump for a flushing mechanism. The tent gave enough privacy and, since it was well ventilated, I imagine it wouldn't stink too bad. The only problem I envisage is that it would be very cold using it. I'm also sorry for the porter whose job was to empty it, clean it and haul it up the mountain every day. After the demonstration, I headed to the trees to do a number one. I thought that it was probably better to only use the toilet for number twos to make emptying easier for the porter.

After nearly an hour, the rest of the group came stumbling into the tent. John and Monique were smiling, but I saw worry on Jamie's face. It wasn't hard to guess that there was something wrong and that she'd found today difficult. We all cheered when we saw them, and said how glad we are that they made it okay. John didn't have his head torch in his daypack, so he'd had to walk right behind Monique so that he could see. We all shared our ordeals, and we were happy at first. Then exhaustion hit, and soon Tania, Anna and Rinze grew quiet. Perhaps the altitude had started to affect them; they all reported having headaches. Anna didn't touch the popcorn, and Rinze almost threw up. Lauren was falling asleep at the table, and could barely keep her eyes open. Then the porters came in with the food, and I hungrily ate. We were served with a proper hot dinner. We had zucchini soup followed by fried fish, spaghetti with no sauce, vegetable stew and potatoes. It was yummy, but Tania, Anna and Rinze had no appetite. It looked like they may have early signs of altitude sickness. But after taking some ibuprofen, they improved enough to force themselves to eat.

After dinner, Herment gave a quick talk on what to expect tomorrow. We have an early start: 6am, and by 7am we need to have our bags packed and then have breakfast. The plan was to set off by 8am. I didn't remember the rest, and as soon as he left, Tania and I said goodnight to everyone. We then walked back to the hut where we'd signed the registration book, since Tania had noticed earlier that there was mobile reception. We managed to make a quick call to the girls. It was lovely to hear their voices, and I'm sure my parents were glad to know that we were doing well. They told us about the terrorist attack, which seemed like it happened ages ago, but in fact was just yesterday. They reassured us that they were fine and they had everything under control. Afterwards, we both crawled into our tent, and I passed out.

Monday, 05 June 2017

I was so tired this morning. I woke up in the middle of the night. When I opened my eyes, I was disoriented, and asked myself why it was so cold, until I remembered that I was in a tent on Kilimanjaro. Then my bladder registered the fact that it needed emptying. I debated whether I could hold it as I didn't want to get up. But the bladder won, so I unzipped my sleeping bag, then put on and zipped up my jacket, unzipped the tent, put on my boots, unzipped the tent canopy, stepped out and finally zipped the canopy back up to keep the mosquitoes out. I went straight for the trees and didn't bother with the toilet tent. After I was done, I went back to the tent and repeated what I would dub the 'zipper symphony': the beautiful sound that the zippers made in the middle of the night when someone had to go to the loo.

The Machame Camp was tight, and all the tents were set up right next to each other. So everyone in our group heard my trip to relieve myself. Afterwards, I had to listen to the zipper symphony several times as they all did the exact same thing. It kept me awake for hours, and just when I was drifting back to sleep, I was woken again by loud radio chatter coming from the ranger's hut. The only words that I could make out were, "Kibo, Kibo, Kibo." The rapid Swahili came in spurts, repeated on four separate occasions. I could only assume that there had been a problem with someone's summit bid and they were radioing for assistance. After that, it was difficult to get back to sleep, and just as I was finally about to doze off, I heard one of the porters offering us some coffee. I ignored it and let Tania get up to speak to him. Eventually, Tania shook me awake and offered me a hot chocolate. I could barely open my eyes, but when I saw her beautiful face, I smiled back. We looked at each other knowingly, and soaked in the fact that we are living our dreams of adventure. She gave me a big cuddle, and that helped energise me enough to get moving and start packing my stuff.

Once we'd packed our duffel bags and sorted our daypacks, we headed to the dining tent, where a warm breakfast was waiting for us. One by one, the rest of the group came in, and everyone seemed to be upbeat. We joked about the zipper symphony, and recounted how much or little sleep we'd had. We all looked tired, but it seemed that everyone had had enough rest to tackle the day. Herment came in to brief us for the day, and told us that we were going to cover about six kilometres; steep up to the halfway point, and then slightly easier.

After eating, we finished our last-minute prep and gathered outside the tents, excited to get going. But before we left, Herment gathered the porters in a semi-circle. I was shocked when I counted twenty of them, plus four guides and two cooks! We were asked to introduce ourselves first, and then they stepped forward one by one saying their names. After the introductions, they started a loud singalong. We watched them perform at least three different songs, while we all joined in the clapping and dancing. It was a real privilege to watch, plus it boosted our morale even further. Out of all the groups at the Machame Camp, our porters and guides were the only ones who did this performance. I saw genuine smiles as they were clearly enjoying themselves. That was lovely and is making our experience that much more memorable.

Once the song-and-dance finished, I was excited to get moving. But then, John told me that Jamie had taken the hard decision to not continue the climb. I was surprised as she hadn't said anything during breakfast and she seemed well enough to continue. We all walked over to talk to her, and she said that her hip was bothering her and she didn't think that she could push through with the pain. Plus, she felt bad for holding the group back. We all took turns consoling her and tried to convince her that she could do it, but it didn't help. I told her about my ten-minute rule, and did my best to persuade her to give it at least ten minutes. Unfortunately, her mind was made up. Tearfully she said goodbye, and went back down with Gaston. It hit me just how hard the challenge was, and I couldn't take it for granted. I briefly wondered how many of us were going to make it to the summit, but quickly pushed the thought out of my mind and focused on the task at hand.

The start of the climb was hard – steep and rocky – but the day was sunny and bright. Soon we were all shedding our layers. Eventually, we settled into a steady rhythm. The beautiful blue sky and the sun gave us the boost we needed after learning of Jamie's decision. It wasn't long before the chatter started again, and we got on with climbing. After a while, I looked back and saw the clouds way below us by the jungle canopy. It dawned on me why it was sunny compared to yesterday. Herment wasn't kidding; I was breathing hard at the beginning of the climb, but it was no problem for the porters, who rushed past us, carrying all the equipment on their heads. It was incredible to watch, and I commented how fit they must be as I gasped for air. For most of the route, we had a clear view of Kilimanjaro. We took plenty of photos at every stop, and I felt that we were starting to gel as a group. We walked together in a single file and got to know each other as the hours went by. During the breaks, we would share around different snacks that we'd brought along – I particularly enjoyed Anna's waffle treats – as well as check on each other to make sure that we're all okay. It was lovely, and I sense the camaraderie and friendship forming.

I used the GPS function on my watch to track our ascent. At each stop, I would give an update on how far we'd gone, how high we'd climbed and how long we'd been walking. It gave us a psychological boost to gauge our progress and calculate how much walking we had left to do. Plus, when I get back home, I will upload the climb to Strava, which I'm sure will get me extra kudos!

Like most of the group, I took out my poles today, so I could use my upper body as opposed to relying solely on my legs. It helped on the really steep sections, and when we got to Shira Cave camp after five hours of climbing, I was relatively fresh and not as tired as I'd expected. The porters had already set up our tents and prepared the dining tent. Inside, an appetising warm lunch was waiting for us: fried chicken and pasta, with boiled eggs and a tasty pumpkin soup. It was delicious, and I stuffed myself. However, the Dutch couple – Anna and Rinze – were still suffering from headaches. When we sat down, I also had a slight headache, but I averted it by drinking loads and loads of water.

After lunch, we had a two-hour siesta. I couldn't sleep, but I enjoyed lying down and resting in the tent. Herment then took us for a short walk to check out the Shira Cave. It wasn't far, and as we stepped inside, I reached up to touch the half dome of the cave. I saw scorched marks on the wall as Herment explained that, in the past, a lot of the porters would sleep there, and would have an open fire inside. I shivered as I pictured how cramped and uncomfortable that must have been. After the short walk, we went back and chilled out around the camp for afternoon tea. We admired the spectacular view and were treated to a gorgeous sunset over the mountain. I was speechless, fully content at the beautiful moment we shared. I soaked it all in, feeling grateful.

At dinner, everyone was in a cheerful mood. I ate loads of the delicious pumpkin soup with rice, plus vegetables and beef stew. Rinze and Anna took painkillers for their headaches, so they were more chatty. There was a lot of laughter, and everyone seemed to be enjoying the experience. Tania and I shared with the group why we're doing the climb and how thankful we were for being able to attempt the challenge, especially with two young kids back home. Then Monique told us that her sister had written her seven letters before she left, and she was supposed to open one for each day she was on the mountain. She shared yesterday's letter, which was a picture of her nephew with a note to say he'll be starting school. That lovely gesture almost made me tearful, as I thought about Sofia and Elisa.

Herment came into the dining tent after dinner and briefed us for tomorrow. Then Tania and I looked for a phone signal, but there was none. But we'd just spoken to the girls yesterday and were glad to hear that everything was all right.

Tonight is colder than yesterday; I hope our sleeping bags will keep us warm enough. The lack of sleep is starting to take its toll. I need a decent snooze.

Tuesday, 06 June 2017

As I was relieving myself before going to bed last night, it dawned on me that we were in the southern hemisphere. I looked up, and found the Southern Cross. It was bright in the sky and the last time I saw the constellation must have been nearly ten years ago. Tania and I were in Brazil, and she was pregnant with Sofia. I thought how fortunate I am to be able to travel, and have an amazing companion to do it with.

I had another awful night's sleep, kept awake by the strong, howling winds. It didn't help that we had another 6am start this morning. Upon waking, we started the routine of getting dressed and packing our sleeping bags into our duffel bags. Last night, Tania commented that I'm starting to smell pretty musky, so I took out the baby wipes and gave myself a mountain wash. I must say that I did smell quite fresh this morning.

Once we'd finished getting ready, I stepped out of the tent, took in the fresh mountain air and immediately felt much better. It was hard not to feel energised by the magnificent, breathtaking view all around us. We made our way to the dining tent, where a hot breakfast lay waiting. As always, the banter was pretty funny, and we were all getting comfortable with one another.

While we were eating, we listened to Herment's briefing for today. The first part was a seven-kilometre hike to Lava Tower Camp at 4,500 metres above sea level, where we'd stop for lunch. We would gain a significant amount of altitude, since Shira Cave Camp was at 3,750 metres. However, we wouldn't be keeping it as we'd do another four kilometres and descend to Barranco Camp, at 3,900 metres. The idea was to spend some time at a higher altitude to allow our bodies to acclimatise and then come back down. We're following the climbers' maxim to 'climb high and sleep low', to help prevent altitude sickness. I understand the theory, but it still seemed like we would be backtracking, and wasting all the altitude gains we would make. But I put it out of my mind, and just went with the flow. Fortunately, all of our legs were fine, and none of us were having any problems climbing.

Before we left camp, we were entertained once again by singing and dancing from our porters and guides. The whole group joined in and we danced away to their lively songs. Everyone loved it, especially the crew. I know that their jobs couldn't be easy, but at least it looked like they all love being up on the mountain. I'm really glad that we picked an awesome company, and we were the only group that sang and danced in the morning. In fact, while we were bouncing to the beat of a Swahili tribal song, I noticed that other climbers from different climbing companies were watching us and also loving our mini tribal rave.

Energised by our mini dance party, we started our hike. The route wasn't as steep as yesterday's, but it was a steady climb. The landscape was rocky and barren, with scarce vegetation. I guess at that altitude, barely anything could survive and grow. The hike was extremely pleasurable, and I'm really happy that we are climbing with a group, and we are all getting on well. If it was just me and Tania, it would have been a completely different experience.

In the group we have John, who is a twenty-five-year-old American. He is talkative, and relishes telling everyone his stories and sharing his past adventures. Lauren is twenty-seven, American, and John's friend. They came with Jamie, and know each other from university. However, they live in different cities now and hadn't seen each other for some time. Lauren seems pretty quiet so far and hasn't shared much. But tonight we learned that she has recently broken up with her girlfriend and, after this trip, will be moving to a different city. I was surprised to learn that she's a lesbian as I originally thought that perhaps John and her might get together. She was sharing a tent with Jamie, but after Jamie left, she didn't mind sharing with John, which led me to think that they might end up hooking up. But upon learning that Lauren likes girls, it made more sense to me.

Monique is a twenty-nine-year-old Maori. She originally introduced herself as an Aussie because that's where she grew up and currently lives. She's travelling by herself, and during dinner this evening we learned that she has a fiancé back home. However, she's not sure what the status of their relationship is at the moment. Coming to Africa had been her dream, but her fiancé didn't want to come and didn't want her to go either, so she moved out of their house and back in with her parents. Monique is a huge laugh and has a positive attitude. She's such a morning person, and always cheerful at breakfast. During dinner, she shared an incredible story. She had been following this South African photographer on Instagram that she secretly has a crush on. He's travelled everywhere, and she loves looking at his travel photos, which inspired her to travel to Africa. Then last week when she was in Rwanda doing a gorilla safari, she randomly ran into him. Her big crush was all of a sudden standing in front of her. At first, she didn't know what to do, but eventually she mustered the courage to tell him how she'd discovered his photos on Instagram, which was part of the reason why she was here in Africa. They chatted for a while but eventually had to say goodbye. It's such a lovely story, and the romantic in me can't help but think that perhaps that was just the beginning of their tale.

Finally, we have Anna, who is twenty-nine, and Rinze, who is thirty years old. They are a married Dutch couple, but no kids yet. Anna seems the more adventurous of the two, and it was her idea to climb Kilimanjaro. Rinze has been quiet so far, but I think that's because he's not dealing with the altitude as well as everyone else. I can tell that they're a good couple and they look like a solid team. I'm looking forward to finding out more about them.

So that's our Kili group, and we're really glad to have ended up with such cool people. Being four years older than Tania makes me the oldest person in our group, but I don't feel like it. I guess I see myself as being the same as everyone else, but with a tiny bit more life experience. I make an effort to ensure that everyone is doing okay, but the cool thing is that everyone watches out for each other, and we're constantly encouraging one another.

We are led by the assistant guide, Anton, who doesn't say much but is extremely strong. He has this slow, steady stride with a precise rhythm, and it seems extremely efficient. When I was walking behind him, I could sense his energy, and by following his steps, it seemed easy-going. John refers to him as our Yoda. The only problem with walking behind Anton is his distinct aroma, which is pungent and hard to get used to. But I'm sure after a couple more days we'll all smell just as bad. Thankfully, we're now high, and it's cold for most of the day, so all our extra layers prevent our bad body odours from wafting through the air. Plus, I kept my neck buff close at hand, so when the stench got too bad, I could easily cover my nose. Today it wasn't much of an issue, and I savoured the fresh mountain air.

We all walked together in single file. It seemed like we were pushing and pulling each other up the mountain. To pass the time, I adapted a drinking game wherein one person would start with, "I went to Kilimanjaro and bought a…" and then name an item starting with the letter A. Then the next person would repeat the list and add one beginning with B, and so on in alphabetical order. I found it entertaining and this is what we came up with:

> *I went to Kilimanjaro and bought an apple, a banana, a circus, a drink, an elephant, a frog, a goat, a helicopter, ice cubes, a jeep, a Klondike bar, livestock, men, nicotine, an octopus, Peter Pan, Quasimodo, a red dress, sun cream, a TV, an umbrella, a vibrator, women, an X-ray, yellow fever tests, and Zanzibar.*

The list was telling of our psychological state at the time. It was an amusing game, and we all got into it. Shortly after we finished, we reached Lava Tower, to eat our lunch. We had been walking on what was called an alpine desert. At an elevation of 4,600 metres, nothing grew up there. I looked at my watch and told the group that we'd been walking for four hours and twenty-three minutes, to cover seven kilometres. Then looked up at the tall tower of rock that dominated the camp, which I guessed was formed by the old volcano. Herment described how it was formed, but I didn't quite hear his explanation. I just admired the beauty of the place, like some alien landscape.

Tania, Anna and Rinze had been having problems with the altitude, suffering bad headaches and nausea since day one. At Lava Tower Camp, I started to experience the same headaches. It wasn't bad at first, and I thought it would go away after I ate and drank more water, but it didn't. It got progressively worse throughout the afternoon until we reached Barranco Camp, where we were camping for the night. The walk down to Barranco from Lava Tower was not pleasant, partly due to my headache. But mostly due to the downhill being quite steep in places, which I found harder on my knees and quads. It was rocky, so I had to be careful with each step. Falling was not an option. Thankfully, after about two hours of descending, we reached Barranco, which was 3.5 kilometres away.

We were relieved to get there, and I immediately took some ibuprofen to help with my headache. Once the pills took effect, I relaxed and soaked up the view. Barranco Camp is so beautiful and seems a bit like a ski resort, but with tents as opposed to bars and restaurants. The peak of Kilimanjaro looked a lot closer, towering over us. Our tents were set up away from most of the other groups, to give us some space. One advantage of going earlier in the season is that it isn't as busy, so we can spread out and enjoy most of the trail to ourselves. We had time to admire the scenery before it got dark, and Tania and I called the girls briefly.

Dinner was delicious, but all of us were looking quite tired. Headaches are now widespread, and we were all on ibuprofen, except for Monique. The altitude hasn't affected her much, probably due to her gym in Australia having an altitude-training room. She trained at a simulated altitude of about 2,500 to three thousand metres, which helped her to acclimatise more easily. As usual, Herment briefed us for tomorrow, when we have to tackle the Barranco Wall. I didn't pay much attention and just thought about getting a good night's rest.

The proud, majestic and standing tall... Toilet Tent

Wednesday, 07 June 2017

Finally, I got some decent sleep. Wearing my fleece to bed helped, and putting my down jacket underneath my sleeping bag for extra warmth. I also slept with my toque on, which kept me warm and toasty. As promised before I fell asleep, I pictured all the people who donated to my charity and gave them all positive shout-outs and a massive thank you.

The solid night's rest was quality, although there was another pee party at two in the morning. It seemed like all of us went to the loo one after another, as if it were choreographed. However, I managed to get back to bed right away, and I wasn't awake for long, unlike the previous nights. I felt fantastic this morning, and most of the group did as well. I guess we're all getting used to sleeping in the tents and the cold temperatures. Either that or sheer exhaustion is shutting down our bodies.

The day started with a lot of energy, and once again we joined the staff in our song-and-dance ritual. Again we attracted looks from the other trekkers, and some even joined us. Our performance seemed to be getting longer and longer, but we didn't mind at all since it was so much fun. However, it also meant that we were always one of the last groups to leave camp. Before we set off, I gazed at the massive Barranco Wall, our first challenge for the day. From where I was standing I could barely make out the long line of climbers who were already on the wall. They looked like ants crawling up it. It was hard to believe that we too would attempt to ascend the massive rock face. We were all excited, but I could sense everyone was nervous at the same time.

It was cold and icy when we set off. The sun hadn't reached the valley floor yet. We were told to put our poles away and use our hands to scramble up the rocks. From a distance, Barranco Wall looked like a sheer rock face, and I was alarmed that we didn't need a harness and ropes to climb it. However, when we got close, it didn't look too bad, and it was fairly safe, although we still had to watch each step and there were points where the guides had to hold our hands to ensure there were no accidents. The wall was only 257 metres high, but enough to churn stomachs when you look down in some parts. The climb wasn't easy, and I was somewhat scared as well as excited scrambling up the rocks, with my heart beating fast. About two hours later, and after a couple of breaks – mainly to let the porters get past us – we eventually reached the top of the wall.

The view was spectacular! All we could see was a sea of fluffy white clouds below us; like standing outside an aeroplane. It was absolutely incredible and exhilarating, as I considered it an achievement to get up there. Funnily enough, there was mobile reception up there too, so Tania and I dialled home. It was lovely hearing the girls' voices, although, Sofia told me that she was sick and didn't go to school. But my mom reassured me that it was only a fever, and we thought perhaps it was because she missed us or was worried about us. My dad then got on the phone and told me that there had been a power outage last night and the Internet wasn't working. I then had to walk him through rebooting the Wi-Fi while I was on top of the Barranco Wall! The last thing I'd thought I would be doing on Kilimanjaro was providing tech support to my dad, but there I was, over four thousand metres high, guiding him through it. It was essential that I got the Internet working again because otherwise they wouldn't get the daily email updates that our tour operator was sending about our progress. More importantly, Sofia and Elisa wouldn't be able to watch Netflix, which I imagine was the only way my mom could handle both of them. Five minutes later, I managed to get my dad to reboot the Wi-Fi and get the Internet working again. As I switched off the phone, I wondered if I was the first person to provide tech support on top of the Barranco Wall. I smiled as I walked to join the group for some photos.

After the break, we carried on walking, and it was mostly downhill. After about an hour, I was baffled to see the next camp. I'd thought the day was going to be much longer, so initially I was glad when we spotted it. However, our anticipation for an early rest was crushed when we realised that Karanga Camp was on the other side of the valley. The camp was nearly level with where we were standing, so we had to climb down to the valley floor first and then back up the other side. It was disheartening, but we just got on with it. The descent was steep, and I went down carefully, mindful of my knee. Most of us had our poles out, and for a while I was cheerily going down slalom-ski-style, using more of my quads to absorb the impact, which made it easier on my knees. Plus, I could lean into the poles to lessen the weight on my legs. But not everyone found the descent as enjoyable as I did. Monique's confidence was shaken early on when she fell. She was behind me, so I didn't see it happen, but she was visibly rattled. Luckily, she wasn't hurt and managed to carry on. Lauren, John and I also had minor slips, but again, we weren't hurt, apart from a slightly bruised ego on my part.

I was knackered when we reached the bottom of the valley from the immense amount of concentration needed to get down. The path was rocky, and I had to be completely focused the whole way. Sadly, there was no respite when I looked up to see the same steep climb back up the other side to reach Karanga. After a brief rest, we all dug deep and just got on with it, one foot in front of the other, and made our way slowly back up. The gradient was steep, and for once I saw some porters struggling behind us. Most of the time they zoomed past, but I guess after four days on the mountain the tiredness was taking its toll on them too. But not everyone was tired, because three-quarters of the way up the last climb, we caught the distinctive smell of weed. Two porters were sat puffing on some Mary Jane and singing 'One Love' by Bob Marley. That brought a huge smile as we all sang along. A terrific way to finish today's hike. Soon after, we reached the top and arrived at Karanga. I looked at my watch and told the group that it had taken us about four-and-a-half hours to cover six kilometres.

Karanga Camp is just spectacular. Again, we were treated to breathtaking views of endless fluffy clouds that stretched far into the horizon below us. It was surreal to think that we are far above the clouds. I have to say, I don't think I've ever had a more beautiful view while taking a pee: gorgeous sunshine, with the majestic mountain behind us. Kilimanjaro looms large, we are getting closer to our goal.

As soon as we got to the camp, we had our lunch. I had another headache, but took ibuprofen, which banished it like a light switch. Over lunch, we shared a lot more jokes and plenty of laughs. We were bonding like a family after being so close during the past couple of days. While we were eating, we shared our travel stories, and I recalled the time I went to Nice, France, for a weekend.

For my birthday several years ago, Tania had got us tickets to see Coldplay in Nice. However, her mum had planned to go to Italy at the same time, so we didn't have anyone to look after the girls. Therefore, Tania couldn't go, so I went on a solo mission to France and stayed in a hostel. It was raining when I arrived in Nice, so I decided to check out Cannes, which was only a short train ride away. As I arrived, I realised that the Cannes Film Festival was on, and checked if I could catch a film. But I didn't know where to go, so I approached two girls who were standing at the barriers and asked them how I could get tickets for a film. They looked at me like I was crazy, then replied that I couldn't just buy tickets; all tickets were given to guests. I thought, *there goes my idea*, and was about to walk away, but before I did, I asked them what they were doing standing by the barriers. They said they were waiting for a friend's dad that might have tickets for them. It turned out, they had been in Cannes for the past four days and had been trying desperately to score tickets. That day they thought they might have a chance. Astonishingly, moments later a man showed up and handed them four tickets. The girls chatted between themselves, then turned to me to ask if I wanted to join them and watch the film!

Of course, I said yes, and we hurried since the film started in five minutes. They told me that usually, the festival organisers print more tickets than there are seats available. Once the theatre is full, they won't let anyone else in. So we started running, and had to go through three security checks. We managed to get past all of the checkpoints, but by the time we got to the theatre, it was full and we were turned away. We were gutted, and I followed the girls back out of the festival, hugely disappointed. After we exited, they said goodbye and left. I then said to myself, *hang on, I just managed to get into the festival with the ticket they gave me, so why have I just walked out?* I still had the whole afternoon to kill, so why not go back in and see what the festival was all about? With the ticket in my hand, I ran back to see if I could get in again. I was nervous, but I thought if I rushed and pretended that I was late for a screening, the security people might wave me through again. Sure enough, I managed to blag my way past the three security checkpoints and then walked to the main hall of the Cannes Film Festival! I was surrounded by the glitz and glamour as soon as I stepped inside. Sticking out in my T-shirt, shorts and flip-flops. People were handing out glasses of wine and all sorts of treats, and I kept looking around to spot celebrities as I wandered about. As I explored, I found the main theatre where apparently, just a day before, Brad Pitt had stood on the same red carpet that I was on. I wondered around for hours and eventually got bored of the free booze and canapés.

But my story didn't end there: the following day, I met an Aussie guy who was working on one of the yachts. He had a day off, and was off to check out Monaco. I asked to tag along, and we took a bus from Nice. It was a beautiful ride along the coast with stunning scenery. He pointed out one of the villas, which he claimed was owned by Bono. When we got to Monaco, we hit the jackpot. It turned out that the Formula One Grand Prix was on that weekend and all of the teams were already there setting up. I couldn't believe my luck, since I'm into Formula One. I'm a huge fan of Lewis Hamilton, and I follow the sport closely. Monaco is one of the most iconic and special tracks on the Formula One calendar, and it's the race that all drivers want to win. The race takes place around the city, and it's one of the few races where the cars race down the city streets. And since they can't close the whole city for the race, the public is free to walk around the circuit. I even wandered into the Paddock Club, where the teams had set up their garages. It was a fantastic treat and such an experience. Monaco and the Cannes Film Festival were so awesome that seeing Coldplay the following night was like an afterthought.

I enjoyed sharing that story during lunch today, and I appreciated listening to their stories too. After we ate, we had a siesta in our tents. I gave myself another wet-wipe bath, which led to Tania and me getting a little frisky, and we enjoyed a quickie before falling asleep. Then, just before dinner, Herment took us for a short hike, so that we could acclimatise some more. We walked up to about four thousand metres, stayed there for half an hour and then walked back down. Monique was extra careful on the way back to camp as she didn't want a repeat fall, but Lauren and Anna had no fear and practically ran down. Thankfully, we all made it back all right. Before dinner, we sat around outside and soaked in the view. The clouds below were mesmerising, and looked like a wave that was frozen or in slow motion. At dinner, there were plenty more jokes and laughs, and it seemed like we were all high, which we were in a sense. Again, I'm so grateful to have such an awesome group. Life is good. Thank you, thank you, thank you.

Thursday, 08 June 2017

This morning was the best start we've had so far. I had an excellent night's sleep, and while packing up the tent I put on some music which lifted my mood even more: a playlist I have on my phone titled *Howie's Reflections*. I made it before coming to London, and since then it has been the soundtrack to all of my travels with Tania. As we were getting ready, it was the perfect time to play it. Since all our tents were clustered together, the music was shared by the whole group, and we even had a singalong to Manu Chao and Bob Marley. It was such an awe-inspiring moment, singing as we gazed out to the beautiful horizon peppered by little fluffy clouds. I loved our time at Karanga Camp, and it is my favourite camp so far.

After breakfast, we had another energetic song-and-dance with the staff. It was a party atmosphere, and I danced and sang like I was at a tribal festival. Tonight is summit night, and I sensed an extra buzz in the air. There was excitement with a hint of apprehension as we will face our biggest challenge when we make our bid for the summit. After our small party we set off for Barafu Camp, also referred to as Base Camp. Most routes up Kilimanjaro use Barafu as the last camp before the summit.

It was a short four-kilometre hike to Barafu, which is situated at 4,673 metres. It took us about three hours to get to the camp. When we did, we saw a lot of climbers just returning from the summit; they all wore a look of pure exhaustion, but serene contentment at the same time. I smiled at them but didn't attempt to make any conversation. They probably just wanted to collapse in their tents.

As soon as we got to camp, we had our lunch and were told to get some rest as soon as we were done eating. We had a few hours for a nap, then we were to have an early dinner so that we could try to sleep for several more hours before summit night. The plan is that we will set off for the summit at around midnight, and it should take us about seven hours to reach the peak of Kilimanjaro just in time for the sunrise. I didn't think too much about what we had to do and how long it was going to take. Instead I focused on what I needed to do first.

Everyone was apprehensive during lunch, and the main discussion during the briefing was about what to wear. Herment told us that we should have at least three layers for our legs and four or five for our upper body. The temperature is expected to drop to −18°C; needless to say, it would be bloody cold! We also discussed taking Diamox to help with altitude sickness, and everyone decided that they would do so. Tania had done the research, and told me that we needed to take one at lunchtime and another at dinner. Apparently, it could reduce the symptoms of altitude sickness, such as headaches, tiredness, nausea, dizziness and shortness of breath. There are some side effects, but I decided not to enquire and just took the pills.

Tania and I didn't have any insulation on the hose for our hydration bladders, so I'm pretty sure that they'd freeze tonight. To deal with this, I made my own insulation by wrapping my wool socks around the hose and taping it up. It looked like it might do the trick, fingers crossed.

We attempted to nap in the afternoon, but it was no use. The air is thinner, and my breathing feels different. I was also too excited and anxious to sleep, so I just lay there with my eyes closed. After several hours, we got up and prepared our packs. At dinner, none of us had any appetite, partly because we'd just had lunch a short while ago. It didn't take long for Herment to burst into the dining tent and advise us to eat more. He said that it was important that we eat as much as we could because we would need all the energy we could get. Reluctantly, I forced some food down. Once we finished eating, Herment, Anton and Goodlove walked in. Herment explained that Goodlove will be walking with us tonight – normally he stays behind to organise the porters. Then they sang a lovely song. Earlier, we had asked if it was possible to do a song-and-dance before we set off for the summit, but I guess the other staff and everyone else at the camp would be sleeping, so it wasn't practical. Still, this was a nice way for them to fulfil our request. The song-and-dance sessions have been an amazing part of our trip so far, and we are so grateful to our guides for making such an effort to make our trip a memorable one.

After we walked back to our tent, Tania and I got into our summit clothes and into our sleeping bags. We now have a few hours to try and get some sleep. The plan is to get up at 10.30pm and set off at 11.30pm. The summit awaits.

Friday, 09 June 2017

I didn't know what summit night would be like, and I started to read about it from my guidebook. But I decided that ignorance was bliss and stopped reading. All I remembered was that it would take us around seven hours to cover about five kilometres to reach the top.

As planned, we got up last night at 10.30pm. Although, none of us slept. Rather, we just lay in our sleeping bags with our eyes closed. I was weary, and drowsy when I got up, but as soon as I stepped out of the tent, the frigid air slapped me in the face. It certainly woke me up. We were told that the temperature could drop as low as −20°C, and it seemed like we were close to it. Tania and I had enough layers on and were reasonably warm. She'd even given me some foot warmers, and they certainly did the job. Apart from the cold, the weather was perfect. It was a clear night, with a full moon and only a little wind.

I had some hot chocolate and biscuits before setting off, but I didn't eat too much. The group looked tired, and subdued. After the warm drink, we set off at 11.30pm, and for once we left on time. Right from the beginning, I found the climb difficult. Anton set a slow pace, but I still found it hard to breathe due to the thin air. It seemed I wasn't getting enough oxygen, and I was uncomfortable. I was walking behind Tania, and she was listening to music. She'd planned a whole playlist for summit night, and it was working for her; she was even dancing at the beginning. That annoyed me somewhat because I thought she should be saving her energy, but then I reasoned that I was just jealous since the music was giving her energy and I was struggling.

In the first couple of hours, we saw a lot of dazed and confused climbers being escorted back down by their guides. It was disconcerting as they could barely walk, and their guides looked worried. The thought of having to turn around and being unable to continue – evidently a real possibility – was very unsettling.

I had no reference points to confirm that we were making progress and we didn't seem to be moving at all. The full moon was bright, but it was still dark, and the only ground I could see was the bit illuminated by my head torch. When I looked up I could see the torches belonging to the group above us, and to my right was Mount Mawenzi, and to my left the silhouette of the mountain's gradient against the dark sky. This view remained constant for hours on end, and it seemed I was walking in the same spot without going anywhere. It was demoralising and mentally difficult.

At dinner last night Tania mentioned that the guidebook recommends farting a lot when climbing. Apparently, this means that your body is adjusting to the altitude, so it's highly recommended for acclimatisation. I now know that this is true since I was breaking wind every five minutes during the climb. I was sorry for Anna, who was walking directly behind me. It probably made it even harder for her to have to endure my stinky flatulence. I just hoped that she had her balaclava on to protect her nose.

It wasn't long before everyone was quiet. The usual banter and chatter were gone; a sure sign that everyone was finding the climb difficult. The only joke came from Rinze, who commented that, "It only took over five thousand metres to shut the Americans up!" It was said in good humour and made us all laugh briefly. The climb was so gruelling, even laughing was an effort. Eventually, the guides started collecting up the girls' daypacks. It was incredible to see each guide carrying two packs weighing at least nine kilos along with their own. At first, my ego didn't want to surrender my backpack, but Anton could see that I was struggling and eventually just took it from me. It made a huge difference, but I still couldn't believe how he managed to carry four packs on his own. I was worried about not being able to drink water regularly without my pack, but the point was moot since I couldn't drink from my water bladder anyway. My makeshift hose insulation didn't work, and the hose had frozen. I had to take out my spare bottle during the breaks.

After a while, doubts set in, and I started to think that it was impossible to continue. The question that kept entering my brain was, *Why are we doing this at night?* It's hard to pull an all-nighter when I'm out clubbing, let alone climbing the highest peak in Africa. I mean, the steep climb was harsh enough, but why did we need to do it in the middle of the freaking night? Surely the sunrise can't be that good! It was hard to push the negative thoughts out of my head, so I focused on my breathing. I tried shutting out the negativity by doing big, deep belly breaths and then forceful exhalations that sounded like Darth Vader. That worked for a bit, but then the negative thoughts came back, and all I could think about was lying down and going to sleep. The climb was relentless and seemed never-ending. I used all my mind powers, including speaking aloud a mantra that went, "It's all good, we're fit and strong." I repeated it over and over, and it did help somewhat.

At one point, I sensed that my body was about to bonk. Evidently, the small amount of biscuits wasn't enough fuel. So I had to force myself to eat some bars, which helped briefly, but not much. Monique was the first to have problems, followed by Lauren. We were all struggling, but they had to stop a lot more. We were so exhausted that none of us was able to offer any encouragement. All we could do was focus on ourselves, save our energy and let the guides help them. The problem with stopping was that, as soon as we stopped, it seemed to take twice as much effort to get moving again. Then the wind started howling and it felt like we'd be blown off the mountain, although apparently it was relatively mild. Herment said that sometimes it got so windy that they had to stop and hug a rock to avoid being blown off. I couldn't even bear to think how much harder it could get. Surprisingly, Tania was taking the climb relatively well. Although she'd stopped dancing, she still had her headphones on, and it was clearly working for her.

As we slowly progressed, I remembered Tania reading from the guidebook about summit night. There was a passage that said to try and ignore the sobbing around you. Then right on cue, I heard a lady from another group, crying her eyes out; she probably knew that the mountain was about to beat her. It must have been at that point that I said to myself that there was no way I was going to quit. The only way I would turn back now was if they carried me back after I collapsed. I would just put one foot in front of the other until I passed out or reached the top.

Just when I thought I had reached my limit, the guides pulled out a thermos of hot tea and forced us to drink it. That break came at the right moment because I thought I was going to black out. At that point, I didn't think that I was going to make it, and I had to dig deep to continue. The steep slope was relentless, and I was hanging on by a thread. I thought that the mountain would beat me. The exhaustion, sleeplessness, bitter cold, gusty wind, steep gradient and lack of oxygen were too much to bear. I was running on fumes. Then I noticed the sky was not as dark, and that gave me hope. I thought that if I could hold on until dawn, maybe I'd make it.

Finally, after about six hours of punishing climbing, we crested the crater and reached Stella Point. I was elated, and had to contain my sobs as I hugged Tania and the team. I let out a big cry when I hugged Herment, and sobbed quietly for a few seconds. I couldn't thank them enough for getting us there. Getting to Stella Point almost broke me, and it was by far one of the toughest things that I had to endure.

While hugging Anna, I remember reading somewhere that Stella Point was named after an Irish woman, who was one of Kilimanjaro's early explorers. Estella Latham and her husband reached the Kibo Crater in 1925 but could not go any further, and so they turned back. They named the pinnacle 'Point Stella' by leaving a note in a glass jar. From Stella Point, it would take another forty-five minutes to reach the roof of Africa: Uhuru Peak. As I let go, I knew that we would go further than Estella and her husband.

Then I found a rock and sat down. I was spent, and it took quite a while to compose myself and recover. Herment and Anton passed around more cups of tea, and the warm drink slowly gave me energy. By that time, daylight was starting to creep in, and the breaking dawn gave us all encouragement. After we gathered ourselves, we set off for the final push to the summit. I was running on empty, but the thought of being so close to the peak gave me an extra push. The gradient of the climb from Stella Point to Uhuru Peak was not as steep as what we had just covered, and felt more relaxed.

As it got brighter and brighter, I noticed the glacier, and the views around us were spectacular. The vista was breathtaking both figuratively and literally. Then as the sun was about to rise above the horizon, I saw the sign for Uhuru Peak in the distance. The floodgates opened, and I started crying. All my emotions came out, and it was one of the most overwhelming experiences of my life. I let the tears flow freely as we continued to walk towards our goal. I must have started it because it wasn't long before I heard Monique and Lauren doing the same behind me. I had the biggest smile as tears of joy streamed down my cheeks. Tremendous relief and accomplishment came over me. All at once I felt excited, elated, grateful and content. I found a sense of communion with myself. During the last few moments before reaching the peak, I was so thankful that we'd managed to get there, and how I would always strive to be a better husband, a better dad, a better son, a better friend and a better person. I repeated my mantra – "Life is good. Thank you, thank you, thank you!" – all the way to the top.

We reached the summit, then I dropped my poles to hug Tania as tight as I could and melted into her. I couldn't believe that we were standing on Uhuru Peak and had made this most incredible journey side by side. I kissed her deeply and said, "I love you and thank you." Hand in hand, we looked around the enormous horizon and watched the sunrise together, soaking in what we had accomplished. We'd known it would be hard, but it was worth it. At 5,895 metres, we were on the roof of Africa, the highest point in the whole continent – how fucking cool is that?!

All of us had a moment up there, and we went around giving each other big celebratory hugs. A lot of photos were taken, and we had a group hug along with our superhuman guides, Herment, Anton and Goodlove. They were brilliant, and it was thanks to them that we'd all managed to get to the top. After waiting our turn to get our photos taken with the famous Uhuru Peak sign behind us, we started making our way down. Sadly, the euphoria of reaching the summit didn't last long, as we soon realised that we still had a three-hour descent back to camp! What goes up must come down, and this thought brought me right back to reality. We were all exhausted, and the thought of having to walk back down almost had me crying again. The route back was as steep as on the way up, and most of it was on loose scree. My boots dug in with every step, almost like walking on snow. It was slow going and agonising. I was utterly drained, and at one point I almost made a treacherous mistake and lost my footing. I avoided falling by using my poles, but in doing so I pulled my right quads and I was in pain. It got progressively worse, and I had to avoid putting weight on it.

The climb down seemed endless, and I don't know how we all managed it, but eventually we stumbled back to camp at around 11am. We were told to take a forty-five-minute nap and then we could have our lunch. Then we had to pack our bags and begin another hike down the mountain towards our previous camp. We marched like zombies and collapsed in our tents. I was beyond exhausted, and just felt numb. I quickly drifted off to sleep, and was instantly woken again for lunch.

The guides knew exactly what they were doing, with the brief rest just long enough to get me moving. If they had allowed us to rest longer, I imagined that none of us would have got up. Our muscles would have seized, and we probably wouldn't be able to move. The warm lunch was filling, and gave us enough energy to tackle the hike down to the next camp. Not long after we set off, we passed an area where these weird-looking devices were parked; like a narrow bed of metal, with one wheel in the middle attached to shock absorbers. Herment said that they're used as stretchers to bring people down the mountain as quickly as possible. Two guides are needed, one at each end, and they can run down the mountain if necessary in an emergency. When we heard that, we all wished that we could ride down to camp on the single-wheeled stretcher.

After lunch, we thought we only had to walk another four kilometres. But after checking my watch, we were over five kilometres with no camp in sight. We must have misheard Herment, and in the end we had to walk over eight kilometres and we descended over 1,500 metres in altitude to reach camp. The terrain was rocky, and we had to be extremely focused while negotiating the descent. It was agony as I ended up hurting my right quads several more times, but eventually, we made it to Mweka Camp, where we would be spending our last night on the mountain. My watch said around 5pm when I signed the camp registration, so we had been on the go for about seventeen hours! We were all extremely exhausted, but everyone was in a jubilant mood.

I still couldn't believe that we'd got through summit night and conquered the mountain. The contentment and relief were evident on everyone's faces during dinner. We were all proud of ourselves, and in a way still in shock at how hard today had been. The past few days were like a walk in the park compared to summit night, but the sense of achievement is priceless. During dinner, we attempted to process and describe what we each went through to get to the top. There were a lot of jokes about acclimatisation farts and how the mountain shut the Americans up, but it was all in jest. We were so happy that we'd made it up not just as a group, but as a family. It'll be hard to describe this experience to someone else fully, but I know that I will always have my Kili family to share it with.

The hike down on the last day

Sunday, 11 June 2017

Yesterday was bittersweet. The sense of accomplishment was immense, but leaving the mountain was sort of sad too. I had butterflies in my stomach when I woke up because I didn't want the adventure to end. When I tried to get up, it was difficult as my legs were sore. Summit night, especially the downhill hike, took a large toll on my body. Eventually, we got moving and started packing our bags. Tania and I made a separate pile of stuff that we donated to the guides and porters. Some of the porters were climbing in gear that looked a bit tattered, and I'm sure they appreciated the gesture. Then we went to the dining tent to have our last breakfast with the group and discuss how much we were supposed to tip. We know that tipping is customary on Kilimanjaro, and a major chunk of the guides' and porters' income. Conveniently, the tour company had advised us; plus Tania and I had some spare US dollars, and we happily agreed to give an extra tip to our guides on top of the suggested amount. We owe them so much more, and we couldn't have done it without them.

After breakfast, Herment gave a speech and told the staff their share of the tip. At first, I was worried that they would be disappointed, but I saw genuine smiles, so there was no awkwardness. After that, we had the biggest song-and-dance celebration. We formed a giant circle and they made each of us dance in the middle while they sang us our own individual chants and blessings. It was a wonderful way to spend our last morning together.

Then it was a relatively short 8.5-kilometre descent to Mweka Gate. However, the gradient was still steep for most of it, and my right quads were in pain for much of the time. We were back in the rainforest canopy, and it felt completely different from the previous days. We saw some cute monkeys while we got wet with a bit of rain. Before we knew it, we were down, and we reached the gate in just under three hours. Big smiles and hugs all around, and we all relished our massive achievement. At the gate, Herment quickly did all the necessary paperwork, and soon we were back on the bus and off the mountain.

They took us to an art gallery/tourist shop, where we had our lunch. There were some gorgeous paintings that Tania and I liked, but they cost more than $3,000 US. However, we spoke to one of the art dealers, and he showed us some more pieces in the back. After sifting through most of them, we spotted one that instantly appealed to us. It was a painting of Kilimanjaro in mostly grey tones on canvas, and it evoked the right emotion. We both agreed that it would be a perfect souvenir that we could hang up in our living room to constantly remind us of our triumphant adventure. After some haggling, we agreed on a price that we were happy to pay.

Later, as we were about to leave, I was heading to the loo when an American climber suddenly stopped me and said, "I know that look."

I replied, "What look?"

"The look that says you've just paid too much for a painting. I just did the same."

I laughed. "No, I just have a look of someone who really needs to take a piss! But out of curiosity, how much did you end up paying for your painting?"

He proudly replied, "I paid $2,500! How much did you pay?"

I tried to hide my amusement. "We got the price down to two hundred bucks. You should have haggled! I've got to take a piss; nice meeting you."

I found the whole exchange amusing since the guy looked like the type of person who likes to brag. The look on his face was priceless, and the group found the story hilarious.

After lunch, we had another hour-long bus ride back to the hotel. Anna and Rinze were staying at a different hotel, so we had to say goodbye to them. But they live in the Netherlands, so relatively close to us in London. I'm sure that we'll see them again at some point. The rest of us were staying at our original hotel, and we were all excited to celebrate that night. When we got back, Herment gave us our certificates for reaching Uhuru Peak, and we said our goodbyes to the crew. They have a couple days off to see their families, and then they're back on the mountain again. He said that during peak season, they only spend one night with their families in-between climbs. I'm still in awe of what they do and how they manage to do it.

Over the past few days, I fantasised a lot about getting to our hotel room and having a lovely shower. And boy, that shower felt divine! It's hard to describe that feeling of achievement mixed with relief and finally getting cleansed after a whole week without a proper wash. It was incredible, but even better was the celebratory romp that Tania and I had soon afterwards. Our hotel bed had mosquito netting around it which made it seem like we were in our tent, and it wasn't hard to imagine that we were back on the mountain, but this time our gasping was not due to the altitude.

After a brief nap, we met everyone at the hotel restaurant, where we had a massive meal and a lot of drinks. Jamie joined us, and told us what she'd got up to after returning on the second day. She kept herself busy wandering around Arusha, and did a safari for a couple of days. She was disappointed at not making it to the top since it had been her idea to climb Kilimanjaro in the first place, but she was determined that she would be back to reach the summit one day. We were quite loud last night, and the other guests avoided us. Most of them will be starting their treks today, and I'm sure they'll be back here next week doing the same. We carried on drinking after all the other guests went to bed, and were kicked out of the hotel restaurant, but carried on celebrating by the reception. Eventually, Tania and I called it a night and said goodbye to Monique. She had an early flight to Cape Town this morning. John, Lauren and Jamie have another couple of weeks of travelling and then they'll be meeting her in South Africa.

I have a hangover today, but not too bad. Our flight home is not until this afternoon, so we're just chilling out until we have to leave for the airport. The Americans' flight is around the same time as ours, so we'll be going together. I usually try not to have any expectations when I travel, so that I'm never disappointed. But if I did have any, this trip has definitely exceeded them. I certainly didn't expect to create such a close bond with a bunch of new people. We started last week with just Tania and me, and we finished it by gaining a whole new family.

I'm sure the experience hasn't fully sunk in yet, and it will be months before I digest and process all of it. All I know is that

I'm so grateful that Tania and I were able to do this together, and my smile will last for a long time. Life is good. Thank you, thank you, thank you.

Top of Africa

THE IMPOSSIBLE DREAM

Wednesday, 14 June 2017

There was a brief worry that we might be stranded in Tanzania before heading to the airport. Jamie informed us that there has been an incident in the Middle East. Saudi Arabia, Egypt, Bahrain and the United Arab Emirates cut diplomatic ties with, and banned air travel through their airspace from, Qatar. We were flying with Qatar Airways to London via Doha, and when we tried to check in, we were told that there would be a problem due to the blockade. Thankfully, the airline managed to rebook us on a KLM flight via Amsterdam, and we eventually made it back to London on Monday morning.

My parents managed to hold the fort while we were gone, and were relieved to see us return in one piece. I was thrust right back into work as soon as we arrived, and spent most of Monday catching up with it. I got some sleep on the plane, so I wasn't too tired and was able to get my work done. It's lovely to be home and seeing the girls was the best.

My legs were still sore from climbing down the mountain, and there was pain in my right quads. I spent forty-five minutes on the turbo yesterday to see how it would feel on the bike.

Luckily, it didn't hurt, and I was thrilled by how easy the turbo was compared to previous workouts. Perhaps all that climbing was beneficial for my cycling legs after all. The only problem was that I'd gained some weight on the mountain. I guess I treated the trip a bit too much like a holiday and indulged with the delicious food they served us. In my defence, we were constantly told to eat, to be sure that we had enough energy for the climb. I must've followed the guides' instructions all too well, and I have the extra kilos to prove it.

I woke up this morning still with some pain in my legs, but only when I go downstairs. I thought about skipping my scheduled training, but reasoned that I couldn't slack off and should get back on it, especially if I want to get rid of the extra weight. So I checked the training schedule, which said that I was supposed to run thirty-two kilometres today. Well, I knew that wouldn't be possible since my parents left today to travel around Eastern Europe, so I was back doing my parental duties and didn't have the time. Plus I was still knackered from the trip. But I thought that I would at least run two laps of Regent's Park, which would be about twenty-four kilometres.

After the morning school run, I set off for the park. I was sluggish at first and my legs were heavy. On any slight downhill section, my calves and my injured quads hurt. It wasn't bad enough for me to stop, so the injury might be a strained muscle from all the downhill walking. After settling into a relatively slow pace, the run was lovely. I was still euphoric from our achievement of summiting Kilimanjaro, and throughout the run, I replayed the awesome memories: the magnificent views, the song-and-dance that the crew did for us each day, and the camaraderie of our group. I was smiling, extremely grateful for such an incredibly wonderful experience, which I was fortunate enough to do with Tania. Both of us are still on this extreme high from our accomplishment, and we're exploring how to use it as a driving force for positive changes in our lives.

Reminiscing on our Kilimanjaro adventures, made running twenty-four kilometres go by quickly. Before I knew it, I was back home stretching, after completing the run with a moving time of two hours and twenty-two minutes. Even though the pace was pretty slow, I was quite pleased that I did the distance, and I felt excellent throughout the day.

Thursday, 15 June 2017

When I was on the mountain covered in dust, I imagined how wonderful it would feel to get in a pool and wash the dirt off. Then I thought how weird it was that, by the following week, I would be back in my London life doing my training routine with endless laps of the pool. That thought turned into reality today, as I found myself swimming lap after lap to complete four kilometres.

I knew it would be hard as it would take me over ninety minutes to complete. But as usual, I broke down the workout into four sets of a thousand metres, and that helped. I smiled as I imagined myself swimming the same distance as the trek between Karanga and Barafu Camps. Albeit, it didn't take me as long to swim as it had to climb it. There'd been times when I'd felt mentally and physically tired during the session and desperately wanted to stop. But I eventually finished it and was proud of myself for not cutting the workout short. Perhaps the long days on the mountain have added to my mental fortitude. I wish that it remains as strong when I do the race.

Saturday, 17 June 2017

Today's ride is my longest so far, and I didn't know what to expect. Psychologically, I knew that it wouldn't be a problem, and I was confident that I could do the distance. All week I was knackered, still recovering from Kilimanjaro. I did an easy forty-minute run yesterday, but it was laboured. I took it slow, but due to the heat, it was taxing. I felt fatigued when I woke up yesterday. However, the one thing that I had going for me today was that I had the whole day for training. Tania took the girls to see her parents, so I had the entire day to myself. Knowing that I didn't have to rush home gave me a psychological bonus. The plan called for a 160-kilometre ride, which I calculated to be about six laps around Richmond Park followed by ten laps around Regent's Park. Unfortunately, my calculations were wrong, and it turned out I was ten kilometres short of the target. But I didn't care, as my main goal was just to finish what I had set out to do, and that was a challenge in itself. Before heading out, I visualised the route and I imagined myself completing it. This helped me prepare for the day ahead.

I estimated that the ride would take me about six hours, and planned my nutrition accordingly. However, I tried something different. Instead of eating at set intervals, I attempted to listen to my body and only eat when I felt the need. Based on this strategy, I took five energy bars and five gels with me. In hindsight, it would have been better if I'd eaten at set intervals to make sure that I was taking on enough fuel. There were points when my concentration started to wane; perhaps due to low glycogen levels. In other words, I was probably close to bonking but avoided it by decreasing my effort and eating more gels.

Right off the bat, I was weak. I'd thought that climbing Kilimanjaro would have been helpful for my riding, but I was sluggish turning the pedals. I had a long day ahead of me, so I didn't push it. It was tough knowing what I had to do. Six laps around Richmond Park was not a thrilling prospect. After the first lap, I started to doubt whether I could do six, not to mention another ten of Regent's Park, plus a run afterwards. However, I tried not to focus on the overall workout. Instead, I broke it down again into manageable chunks. With each lap,

I just concentrated on the two big hills that I needed to tackle, then attempted to enjoy the bits in-between as recovery. But even this strategy got tedious, and I had to resort to all sorts of mental gymnastics to keep myself focused. I replayed a lot of our Kilimanjaro climb, which kept me occupied. During the climbs, I'd kept repeating, "*Pole, pole,*" to myself. This helped a lot and made sure that I didn't blow up on the hard uphill slogs.

With patience and determination, I eventually finished the six laps around Richmond, then made my way towards Regent's Park. The sun was still beating down, and by that time the London traffic had picked up. I had to ride slower with traffic, but I didn't mind since I could recover slightly. But by the time I got to Regent's Park, I was drained. My bike computer told me that I had done nearly a hundred kilometres. I had been riding for over four-and-a-half hours, and it was hard to imagine that I still had to do another ten laps. But as always, I pushed the thought away and told myself to concentrate on doing one lap at a time. I thought that after I got the first one out of the way, the rest would be easier. But nope, it didn't happen that way. With each lap, I had to force myself to keep going. My brain kept telling me to stop and go home. It was hot, and I kept imagining a cold shower. But every time my brain told me to quit, I countered by saying that this was what it was all about. I needed to figure out how to push myself beyond what I thought was my limit, overcome the urge to quit and finish the ride. After a couple of laps, I looked over and saw the giraffes and zebras at the zoo. It was the perfect distraction, and every time I rode past them, I said that I would see them again later. From that point onwards, when I thought about quitting, I reasoned that I couldn't possibly keep the giraffes and the zebras waiting and not show up for our date. I was probably delusional and hallucinating at that point, but it worked, and somehow I managed to complete ten laps.

After spending hours in the saddle, I found myself back home. I was hot and exhausted, but my day was not over yet.

After a quick change into my trainers, I forced myself to eat another energy bar, and off I went, curious to see how my legs would function after seven hours of cycling. It wasn't hard to get going as I imagined the run would be like recovery. I was surprised that my legs were fine at the beginning, albeit I was going really slowly. I felt something funny with my left knee, so I stopped several times to stretch and prevent injury. The temperature hit its peak for the day: 28°C! It is rare for London to get that hot, and all I thought about was climate change. Eventually, I found a relaxing and sustainable pace, and finished the run after thirty-seven minutes. I ran the five kilometres with a pace of 6:43/km; not even close to my marathon pace, but I reasoned that if I could hold that pace for the Ironman, I could potentially finish within the cut-off time of seventeen hours. I briefly smiled afterwards, but I was too exhausted to hold it. The brick session took just under eight hours to complete, and it made me fully grasp how tough the Ironman would be. But at the same time, I was pleased with myself for completing the session without cutting it short. The experience has increased my mental fortitude and made me better prepared.

Sunday, 18 June 2017

I woke up with arms wrapped around me from my loving daughters shouting happy Father's Day. They ordered me to stay in bed as they marched downstairs to prepare breakfast. I stared at the ceiling contemplating going out for a two-hour recovery ride as per the training plan, but I just rolled over in my cosy bed instead. I figured I deserved it not only to enjoy my day as a father, but also from the massive session yesterday.

I started yesterday's ride at around 7am, and it was a cool 17°C when I left. By 10am I noticed how hot the sun was getting, and realised that there were no clouds in sight. Looking at my sweaty arms, I thought that I should have put on sunscreen. However, there was nothing I could do as I forgot to bring any. When I took a shower today, it reminded me of my error. My arms and legs were bright red, and the tan lines were defined. Standing naked before the mirror, I looked like I was wearing arm and leg warmers. I smiled as I recalled Rule #7 of the Velominati, which stated that 'tan lines should be cultivated and kept razor sharp',[6] making me think that I'm following the path of the Velominatus, which is the never-ending struggle waged between form and function.

We spent the afternoon celebrating the rest of Father's Day at the park by having a picnic with some friends. I proudly showed off my hideous tan lines to everyone, and boasted about how I got them. I happily bored them about my ride yesterday with a huge grin on my face.

Tuesday, 20 June 2017

It was weird going back to a smaller pool, after getting used to the twenty-five-metre one. It seemed like I kept bouncing between the walls and was going too fast. I had to remind myself to slow down and eventually, I settled into the swim. It was difficult to go at a slower pace, especially after resting for two days. My body just wanted to go full gas. However, I knew that I couldn't sustain the fast pace over 3.8 kilometres.

Yesterday I finally signed up for the five-kilometre open-water swim at Dorney Lake this weekend. It's something I've never done before and was slightly apprehensive; anxious about the unknown. The longer distance should give me important experience and confidence for the Ironman. However, I haven't done any practice swims in my wetsuit this year, which is slightly

---

[6] The Rules by Velominati Keepers Of The Cog: http://www.velominati.com/the-rules/

concerning. Ideally, I should have at least one session in open water wearing it. But I don't have enough time to go out with the wetsuit before the race, so I might swim with it in the pool on Thursday.

Dorney Lake is a rowing lake similar to the Outlaw's swim venue. The five-kilometre course will be two laps around the lake, which should take me a little over two hours. The first triathlon race – a sprint distance – that I did was at Dorney Lake. For that, I only had to swim 750 metres, and it was a struggle. I'd just finished reading *Total Immersion*, and was still teaching myself the front crawl. I came dead last for the swim and barely got around the course, and now I'm going back to swim five kilometres. I'm sure I'll still be one of the last ones in my wave, but at least now I can swim competently enough to know that I can complete the course.

Saturday, 24 June 2017

I set my alarm for 6.30am today, but, as usual on a race day, I woke up way too early and couldn't get back to sleep. I've been visualising the past few days, and I've gone over the whole race in my head many times. I got my stuff ready last night, and since I was only doing one sport today, there wasn't much to organise. I ate my usual breakfast of porridge and toast with almond butter and banana, then headed out the door just before 7.30am. That gave me plenty of time to drive to Eton's Dorney Lake for the 9.30am start. Thankfully, the heatwave has finally ended and we're back to the normal cooler temperatures. It was 18°C and cloudy this morning, and as I drove to the lake there was light rain. I was slightly concerned about the wind, but it wasn't as bad as yesterday.

When I approached Dorney Lake, I noticed the sign announcing that it was an Olympic rowing venue in 2012. With its proximity to Eton and Windsor Castle, the whole venue was properly maintained. When I got there, I went through the usual registration process and chatted with some guys about the swim. There were other races taking place, and waves for 750, 1,500, three thousand, five thousand and ten thousand metres. The five-kilometre event was the last wave, and consisted of two laps. My strategy was simple: I would relax, go slow and maybe find someone to draft behind.

With only about a hundred swimmers in my wave, I knew that, given my slow pace, I would be at the back of the pack. But I didn't mind since my main goal was to get experience for the long-distance swim. I plan to swim at the same pace for the Ironman, and my aim is just to get around the course so that I have enough left for the bike and run afterwards.

Getting into the water was relatively calm compared to the mass start of a typical triathlon. We crossed the timing mats in an orderly manner and set off two at a time. There was no big shock to the system when I got in, as the water felt really warm since the air temperature was cooler due to the recent heatwave. I was worried that people would all of a sudden start to swim over me like in a triathlon, but there was none of it. So early on I got into a nice relaxed rhythm, and, as expected, after about five minutes things started to calm down as the pack swam up ahead and left me behind.

When I sighted, I noticed a couple of other swimmers around me, so I drafted behind one who looked to be swimming at the same pace as me. I got behind him and matched his pace. However, I kept bumping into his leg, and I felt bad for screwing up his rhythm. I soon realised that he was going much too slow for me and I was better off passing him. Later I learned that he'd finished last, and was glad I made the right decision.

After passing the last swimmer from my wave, I settled into a rhythm. Eventually, I was on my own, and lost sight of the pack. I only had the buoys to guide me, and had to rely on my sighting abilities to swim straight. Unlike the pool, where I could see the lane markers at the bottom, all I could see in the lake was a murky green or brown. Following my sighting technique, I looked up a lot more often. Before, I would only look up once in a while when I remembered, by which point I would have veered off course and would have to make a correction, which resulted in swimming in zigzags. But today, I followed my sighting technique that I learned in Greece, and I sighted more regularly, by incorporating it as part of my breathing pattern. Normally in the pool, I would take two breaths in a row on my left and then two on my right. But in open water, I now sight after breathing twice on my left before switching to my right. Breathing bilaterally also helped me utilise both shorelines to gauge my direction. It seemed to work as I was able to hit the buoys along the course.

As I was making my way around, things went smoothly until suddenly my eyes became irritated. There wasn't any water in my goggles, so I couldn't figure out what could be causing the irritation. Then I realised it must have been the anti-fog spray. My current goggles had been leaking, so two days ago I decided to use my old pair. Before setting off, I sprayed the old goggles with some anti-fog solution so they didn't fog up. However, there was no water around to rinse them before the race started, so I used an old trick and just spat into them. But I guess that wasn't enough, and it was causing my eye to irritate. It got so bad that I had to stop, then float on my back in order to clear it. But it didn't work, and my eyes were still hurting, so I swam closer to the shoreline and stood up briefly to clean my goggles properly and wash my eyes out. When I got going again, they didn't hurt as bad. The only problem was that my foot started stinging. I decided to ignore it as the pain was bearable, but when I approached the drink station, I decided to stop to check it out. I saw a small cut on my left foot, which must've been from the rocks while I was clearing my goggles. I made sure it wasn't deep, then took a quick sip of water, and I was off again.

The rest of the race was pretty uneventful apart from being passed and lapped by the faster swimmers who were doing the ten-kilometre race. As expected, things progressed slowly, and it seemed like I wasn't making any progress at all. Eventually, I rounded the last corner and headed for home. In the distance, I noticed two other swimmers who were wearing the same blue swimming caps as I was. It was encouraging as I hadn't seen anyone else from my wave since shortly after the start. I continued steadily and soon realised that the gap between us was getting smaller and smaller. I was catching up with them! But I didn't want to get too carried away, so I kept my head down and continued at my own pace. After a couple more breaths, I looked up to sight, and they were no longer in front of me. I was confused, so on my next breath I quickly looked back and realised that I had passed them. My adrenaline kicked in, as I couldn't remember the last time I'd passed anybody in the water during a race. I picked up the pace and focused on staying ahead of them.

Finally, the finishing buoys were in sight, and I kicked faster. I could hear splashing behind me, and thought that the swimmers I'd passed would overtake me in the end. Instinctively, I swam harder, but it was no use as I could sense his wake alongside and would soon overtake me. I glanced and saw a green cap, then calmed down as I realised he was swimming a different distance. So I let him go and concentrated towards the shore. Before I knew it, I was being helped up by a volunteer and was on dry land again. I crossed the finishing mat grinning ear to ear, then I spotted the cameraman and gave him a broad smile and a huge thumbs up. I looked up in triumph after finishing, and I was ecstatic after finding out that I wasn't last!

My official time was two hours and fifteen minutes, and I came fourth last out of a field of 125 swimmers. My predicted pace based on my pool swim was two hours and five minutes, so at first I was disappointed. But my watch said that I'd swum

5,176 metres, hence my actual pace was 2:29/100m; the same as my pool pace during training. Also, examining the GPS data, it looked like I'd swum relatively straight, and all the other people who uploaded their data to Strava also reported swimming a distance of over five thousand metres. Overall, I was pleased with my time. I also felt relatively fresh after exiting the water, so that was a positive sign for the Ironman next month. However, my eyes started to sting again after I took off my goggles, so I walked to the first-aid tent. The paramedics had a look and said they were irritated and they'd give them a proper wash. Afterwards, it was a bit better, but my eyes were blood-red for the remainder of the day. Later on, I took Elisa and Sofia to a birthday party, and the other parents asked me what had happened to my eyes. I smiled and proudly said that I'd just swum five kilometres!

Sunday, 25 June 2017

I had to move my usual Saturday brick session to today because of yesterday's race. The plan was to cycle 145 kilometres and then run for another fourteen. I knew from the start that this was a tough call, and I doubted that I would complete the distance. Based on last week's brick session, I knew I could cycle that distance; however, I was doubtful that I could complete the run.

Before heading out, I had to spend some time replacing my rear brake pads. They were making a really bad sound, and I'd been meaning to change them for quite some time. It took about half an hour, and judging by the looks of the old brake pads, they should've been changed months ago. They were so worn out that they were down to the metal. The front brakes looked like they need changing too, so I ordered another set of pads. By the time I got out of the house, it was nearly eight o'clock.

The temperature was a cool 17°C; a stark contrast to last week's scorching ride. I planned to do five laps around

Richmond Park and then eleven around Regent's Park. The ride started off ordinarily enough, and I reached Richmond Park in about forty-five minutes as usual. Once I started the first loop, however, I immediately felt different compared to last week. For some reason, I was a lot stronger, and my legs seemed to want to push a lot harder. On the first crack up Sawyer's Hill, I managed to stay on the larger front cog, and I even attacked the end of the climb. It was weird, but I was enjoying the new-found energy. Perhaps the couple of days off as part of my rest week is working. Also, I was sure the cooler weather made a difference, or maybe all the training is paying off. In any case, I was finally getting some cycling form, and I just want it to continue.

I seemed to go faster all the way around the park. I even overtook some people. This is rare for me around Richmond Park, but then I remembered that it is Sunday, so perhaps Sunday cyclists are not as fast as Saturday riders. But it didn't matter; it was awesome passing people and not having to yield all the time. Of course there were still a lot of other guys who passed me, but at least I dished out some overtakes as well.

Round and round I went, and on each lap, I attacked both of the main climbs. Then on my fourth lap, I looked back and saw two riders drafting behind me. I thought they would eventually pass me, or turn and leave the park or something, so I continued with my head down and kept a steady pace. Eventually, we hit the climb, and I was sure that I would get passed, but as we crested the hill, nothing happened. After I caught my breath, I looked back and saw the same guy struggling to get back on my wheel. *Wow!* I thought – I ended up dropping them on the climb. I grinned as I took a swig of water. I carried on at the same pace, and the two guys eventually got back on my wheel. Again, I expected them to come around and pass me, but they didn't. So, for the last two laps, I pulled them around the park, and they happily tucked behind my wheel. It was satisfying to be in front for once, and it made me feel a tiny bit stronger.

After five laps around Richmond Park, I made my way towards Regent's Park. It didn't take me long to get there, as the roads were not that busy compared to a Saturday morning. When I approached the park, I saw a huge number of people were out in the streets. I realised that it was the end of Ramadan, so everyone was out celebrating at the mosque that's by the park. The park gate that I normally use was closed to vehicle traffic, so I had to get off my bike and walk in. It was extremely busy, and the traffic was moving slowly with all the cars trying to park. Cycling wasn't ideal due to the crowd, and it sucked away my momentum. I completed three laps before thinking that there was no point in continuing. So I headed for home and called it a ride. I looked at my watch, and I'd ended up riding 109 kilometres with a moving time of four hours and forty-nine minutes. The elapsed time including all the traffic stops was five hours and fifteen minutes.

As I got home, our guests for the afternoon had just arrived. I said a quick hello and told them that I would meet them at the park for our picnic. Then I was out the door again to start my run. I knew that doing fourteen kilometres was out of the question as I already felt guilty for leaving our guests. So I ended up doing just 7.6 and then called it a day. Even though I didn't complete today's required training, I had a solid session. My legs were strong on the run, and I knew I could've run fourteen kilometres easily. Plus, with my solid cycling legs today and yesterday's five-kilometre swim, it made me get excited about the Ironman. I hope that my excellent form continues and that I stay fit for the next couple of weeks.

Tuesday, 27 June 2017

I took yesterday off to recover from Sunday's brick session, and spent some time looking at the Eton Swim results. My jaw dropped when I found out that the person who came in first did the swim in one hour and eight minutes; about half the time it took me to complete the five-kilometre swim! It got me thinking that there must be a way for me to get faster in the water. I analysed my technique, and concluded that I'm losing some propulsion during the catch/pull phase. This is the phase of the stroke when the arm is underwater, and the swimmer is pulling themselves forward. What I realised during the race was that, in the pull phase of my stroke, my arm was going down as opposed to backwards. Therefore, most of the energy was used in pushing myself upwards as opposed to forwards. As a result, I think I lose a lot of momentum and go slowly.

I've been so focused on completing my swim workouts, that I haven't thought about improving my technique. Now that I know that I can swim the Ironman distance, I need to look at what I can tweak in order to swim faster. As such, last night I did some research on how I could improve the catch/pull part of my stroke. I came away with two things to try, and was excited this morning to see if they would work. The first thing is to push my arm directly backwards as opposed to downwards. I tried to do this by using what swimmers call a 'high-elbow catch'. The second thing is what Total Immersion (TI) coaches refer to as 'spearing'. This is when the leading arm enters the water and creates a long body line that parts the water so that the body can glide through. These techniques are from different schools of thought, and I was keen to find out which would suit me better and, more importantly, make me go faster.

Using the high-elbow catch, I immediately noticed that I could 'grab' more of the water by raising my elbow higher during the catch/pull phase. It seemed I was going faster and using fewer strokes per length, but it also felt like I was putting a lot more effort into the pull. That was probably what was making me go further with each stroke. However, by focusing on pulling directly backwards as opposed to downwards, I was 'catching' more of the water, and it seemed like the right thing to do.

Then I focused on spearing, and immediately I noticed that it took less effort. If I could combine it with the high elbow, I might be on to a winner. The other thing I noticed with the spearing method was the sensation that I was continuously gliding forwards and not losing any of my momentum. Plus, it was easier compared to just trying to 'pull' harder to increase my speed. In the end, I swam 2,100 metres focusing on the combined high-elbow-and-spearing technique. My overall pace was faster, so it was encouraging. My conclusion is that I should put more focus on spearing, but also remember to employ the high elbow for my pull. The goal now is to continue practising this and improving my stroke.

Last night I watched this show about all the different art forms that people practise in Japan. One was ikebana, which is the Japanese art of flower arrangement. Ikebana is more than simply putting flowers in a vase; rather, it is an art form steeped in the philosophy of developing closeness with nature. What resonated with me was an interview with an ikebana master in which he described himself as being on a journey where the path has no end. The main purpose is to learn and improve his art continually. It struck a chord with me, as I've read that swimming could also be described as an art form. It has been over nine years since I started my swimming journey and, although I have progressed far, I am certainly nowhere near the pack, and I still have much to learn. The ikebana master reminded me that I should keep striving towards mastery, improve my technique and never stop learning.

Wednesday, 28 June 2017

I originally thought that I only had to do a one-hour run today, but when I double-checked my training plan, it said that I had to do ninety minutes. I wasn't prepared for the extra half-hour of running, but nevertheless, I planned a route and just set off. I'm in Week 9 of my twelve-week Ironman programme, and after this week the workload will get lighter as I enter the taper phase of my training.

While running, I reflected on my year so far, and suddenly a huge wave of gratitude came over me. I'm so grateful for everything I've done this year. Training day in, day out is difficult at times, but it has been such an incredibly rewarding journey. I'm fortunate enough to enjoy most of it, and to have the time and family support to be able to do it. Today I thought that, whatever the outcome of the Ironman, I'm still more than happy and thankful to have come this far. As I have said, just getting to the start line is a challenge in itself. I have so much respect for everyone who decides to take up a challenge and sets about figuring out how to overcome it; and for those people faced with what seem to be insurmountable difficulties due to circumstances beyond their control, who somehow conquer them. Some of my friends think that I'm crazy for doing the things I do, but I explain that I attempt these challenges to push myself beyond my boundaries and my current abilities. These challenges help me to redefine my horizon, which allows me to learn and grow as a person in the process. Perhaps, there are many treasures hidden within ourselves, and sometimes it takes challenges to unearth these personal riches. Taking myself out of my comfort zone forces me to 'dig deep' within myself and allows me to discover my hidden gems. I've done this by doing sports, travelling, being in a relationship, being a father or just by trying to fully experience life. Seeking these treasures makes life as one big adventure, and makes the journey very exciting.

When people see me, 'athletic' or 'triathlete' are probably not words that pop into their heads. First of all, I'm relatively short being only 5'5" tall. I have a bit of a belly, which I can hide most of the time but which probably sticks out if I'm breathing normally. I guess because I'm short, people are more impressed that I do triathlons and endurance sport. As someone pointed out, I have a small engine to work with, but I believe that my strong mental stamina makes up for my lack of natural physical ability. In any case, I have to work with what I have, and hopefully this will be enough to get me around the course.

These thoughts swirled through my head as my feet pounded the pavement. The run was relaxed, and the cooler weather was lovely. After a couple laps around the park, I looked at my watch and saw that I had done almost fourteen kilometres. I had been running for an hour and twenty-five minutes. Time to stop and savour the cool-down walk home with a lovely smile on my face. Life is good. Thank you, thank you, thank you.

Thursday, 29 June 2017

I was looking forward to getting back in the pool, keen to practise the spearing and high-elbow technique again. Instead of doing twenty laps in a row, I decided to do two laps at a time and experiment with the new technique. At the beginning, I was faster, but this was less to do with the technique and more to do with my effort. The swim felt more laboured, and I knew that the pace was not sustainable over a long distance. Nevertheless, I kept my focus on spearing the water and improving the catch/pull of my stroke.

Towards the end of the workout, I started doing longer sets, and I slowed down the pace. In doing so, I suddenly realised what I have been doing wrong. It seemed that my timing was all off and I was pulling too early with my lead hand. By slowing the pace, I could keep the lead hand forward and not start the pull until I speared with the other hand first. Getting this timing right was key, and it was something that I would need to keep practising. Also, I noticed that in getting the timing right I didn't lose any momentum; I was gaining forward thrust from the spearing motion plus the pulling hand. As a result, even with a slower stroke rate, I was swimming faster but with less energy, and therefore I could sustain the pace for longer distances. It was exciting.

After exiting the water, I kept reminding myself of what I did correctly so that I can continue practising it in my next swim session. In the *Total Immersion* book, the author says that it takes about ten thousand metres of repetitive movement to imprint a new swim technique. With the amount I'm swimming currently, it should take me about a week. I'm looking forward to finding out if it makes a difference.

As it happens, an email landed in my inbox today with the subject line 'Mastery is a Process Where You're Always Working on Improving'. I read this email, and it resonated so much with me and encapsulated what I've been thinking about with my swimming over the past couple of days:

> *Many people think that mastery is a goal to shoot for. In reality, mastery doesn't happen in the future; it happens in the present! It's when you bring to bear everything you know up to that point, to make a single moment the best you can... and to grow from having done so.*
>
> *The Japanese use the word 'kaizen' to describe the art of approaching everything you do with a sense of curiosity that leads to always learning something about whatever activity you're doing.*
>
> (Total Immersion)[7]

Saturday, 01 July 2017

Today was the last long ride in my training programme. I had to do a 144-kilometre cycle and then a 6.5-kilometre run. I was

---

7   Total Immersion email: 'Mastery is a Process Where You're Always Working on Improving'. Received on 29 June 2017 from info@totalimmersion.net

too busy with work to fit in a workout yesterday, but it wasn't a key session, so I figured it should be okay to skip it. I ate a lot of pasta last night, and although I haven't been paying much attention to my diet, I've learned from my KFC bonking and I know that eating the right things before a long workout does help. I felt strong this morning, so I decided that I would do six laps around Richmond Park followed by eight laps around Regent's Park. The weather was perfect; it was about 16°C and overcast when I started, and didn't get any higher than 21°C in the afternoon. The only problem was that the wind did pick up towards the end of the ride, but overall it was fine.

The ride was relatively easy, and I attacked all of the hills in Richmond Park. I was faster than last week, but with less effort. The training is paying off, and my body is now used to the harder workouts. I even contemplated doing more laps of the hillier Richmond Park and fewer of the flatter Regent's Park, but in the end, I stuck to my plan and comfortably finished the 144 kilometres with a moving time of six hours and fifteen minutes. I was held up by a lot of traffic lights, so I know that I could've gone faster. Based on today's time, I think I can complete the bike ride for the Outlaw in under eight hours. It is definitely doable as long as the weather is not too hot and not too windy.

I was relatively fresh after the long ride, and when I got home, both my legs felt good. So I quickly got changed and scoffed down another energy bar for my run. The run started off all right, and I wasn't too tired from the bike ride, which was encouraging. I went faster at the beginning, and had to remind myself to slow down so that I didn't overdo it. Since I was feeling strong today, I decided to extend my run, and I did a couple of laps of the hillier section of my local park to compensate for cutting my long run short last week. I'd thought the hills would be a killer for my legs, but unusually they weren't too bad. I found a pace that was relaxed the whole way around. Eventually, after just over ten kilometres, I decided to call it a day. I could have continued, but it was better to stop. It was a positive sign that I wasn't completely exhausted during the run; it gave me confidence for the race. If everything goes according to plan, it should be possible for me to complete the Ironman within the allowed time.

The best part of training is the post-workout bliss after completing a particularly hard session. I planted myself on the couch afterwards, satisfied to know that I earned it. I flicked through the TV and happily found out that the Tour de France had just started. However, I did miss most of the coverage, as I was soon asleep. I woke up to learn that Geraint Thomas, a Welshman from Team Sky, had taken the yellow jersey in the time trial. I was ecstatic, considering that I'm cheering his teammate Chris Froome to win the Tour again this year. The Tour starting reminded me that it's now July, which means I only have about three weeks left until the Ironman. Having finished the biggest training session, I'm now looking forward to the less intense taper period. Excitement is building for the race, and I have to believe that I've done enough training for it. Not long to wait to find out.

Thursday, 06 July 2017

I was in the pool at 6.30am this morning to get my swim out of the way from my busy day. We had a visit from Elisa's new school where she will be starting in September, and then I had a meeting followed by Elisa's nursery graduation, which was the cutest thing ever. They performed a small play, which was adorable, and it was hard to believe that she's finishing nursery soon and will be starting big school in the autumn. I still find it fascinating to watch my daughters grow up and learn new things. It's one of the most wonderful things for a parent.

Speaking of learning, I continued improving my new swim stroke, and analysing why my right-side breathing is not as smooth as my left. The problem when breathing to my right is that it seems hurried and I'm not getting a full breath, which throws off my rhythm. I worked on it today, but with minimal success. I got it at times, but then I seemed to lose it. I think it'll take several more times before I get it right, but I have to do it soon. I did manage to complete a three-kilometre swim in one hour and nine minutes, and now I'm starting to dream that I can complete the Ironman swim in under ninety minutes.

All of the hard work is almost done now, and I have the taper for the next two weeks after this weekend. My excitement is building, and I'm really looking forward to the race. I'll be chasing another smile in about two weeks' time.

Monday, 10 July 2017

I did a two-hour ride yesterday, and it was meant to be an easy recovery ride. However, once I got to Regent's Park, there was a group of cyclists going at a slow pace, and I figured I would draft behind them to make it even easier. What I didn't realise was that they were just finishing their warm-up, so I was misled by their relaxed pace. The peloton started to pick up the pace, and for some silly reason, I decided to find out how long I could hang on their wheels. As I was panting and breathing hard, I glanced at my bike computer and noticed that we were going at about thirty-six kilometres an hour; way faster than my normal twenty-eight. After two laps, I was dropped from the fast group, but I found another group of four riders that was going slower, so I hung on to them instead. They were still going faster than my usual pace, but I thought it would be exciting to ride with a group for a change. The four guys took turns at the front, and I decided to see if I could do so too, to see if I could keep the pace going. I surprised myself when I managed to do a whole lap around the park holding the same pace while the other guys drafted behind me. It was pretty cool leading the pack, and I was pleased to see that my cycling legs were fast enough to keep up with some riders.

I'm starting to enjoy this taper period. Not only am I supposed to take the workouts easier, but they're shorter too. The next two weeks are going to be great. I just have to make sure that I don't fall at the final hurdle, like I did five years ago, when I was training for a sprint distance triathlon. It wasn't my main race that year but I still trained for it as part of a bigger training program towards an Olympic-distance triathlon. However, things didn't go to plan because a week before the race I went to Prague with Slater for a few days and then we met up with Kyle in Amsterdam for a little boys trip. That was a fun and memorable trip but all the partying negated my training and unfortunately I didn't make it to the start line. But to my credit I still did the race distance on my own. I wasn't too disappointed about missing that race as it was more important to spend time with my friends, plus it wasn't the main race that I was training for. It goes to show that things can still get in the way even if you've completed your training. I just have to stay focused and avoid socialising too much in the next couple of weeks.

Thursday, 13 July 2017

Today was another case where I had to adjust my training due to other circumstances. Elisa has been complaining of a bellyache since Monday evening, so yesterday we decided to keep her at home, and I took her to the doctor this morning. Tania and I were concerned that it might be appendicitis, which I had when I was a kid and her symptoms seemed similar. The doctor was quite confident that it wasn't, but wanted to take a urine sample to test for an infection. He suggested that we give her some paracetamol to help manage the pain until we get the results.

So I hung out with Elisa yesterday and kept her company. I did manage to get a run in before Tania left for work. It was only thirty minutes, and there was no problem getting it done by 7am.

It goes to show the different challenges that an average triathlete must juggle along with training. I count myself very lucky to have a lot of flexibility regarding my time; because of the nature of my job, I can easily shuffle training sessions around. I'm sure that there are a lot of other triathletes, or amateur athletes for that matter, who are not so fortunate and face much harder obstacles to get to the start line.

I've spent the past few nights studying the race route. I've searched the Internet for every bit of information about previous Outlaw events, and there was video coverage of the past few years' events available. I've watched a couple of them already, and they proved a valuable resource for learning the course. I find it useful to see the swim course and the transition set-up, to familiarise myself with them; and to get an idea of the different weather conditions in previous years. I learned what other competitors wore on cold, rainy or hot days. That should help with my preparations, and be fully ready for race day. As they say, there is no such thing as bad weather, just bad clothing. Having said that, I wish that it will be overcast and around 18°C, with no wind. However, I've constantly been checking the long-term forecasts, and as of today it's saying that it'll be mainly cloudy with a scattered light rain and a high of 21°C. Apart from the rain, that's not too bad, and I hope that it's not going to be hot.

Sunday, 16 July 2017

I had a fantastic ride for my last bike session today. I went to Regent's Park for an easy two-hour spin, and I stayed on my aerobars for most of it. I pedalled slowly at a lower cadence since it was supposed to be an easy ride. As I was cruising along, I started passing a few riders around the park. When I looked at my speed, I was pushing more than thirty kilometres an hour, which was faster than my usual pace. I checked my rear dérouiller and saw that I was in a higher gear, but remarkably it still seemed easy. As an experiment, I shifted to an even harder gear to see how long I could maintain it. And surprisingly, I had no problems keeping a pace over thirty kilometres an hour. It was terrific passing people I normally couldn't keep up with. Other riders tried to draft behind me but I ended up dropping them.

Towards the end, a fast peloton went by, and I wanted to see if I could hang on to them. They were going at about thirty-five kilometres an hour; significantly faster than me. Again, it was relatively easy for me to get on their back wheels, and I couldn't believe that I could stay with them for the whole lap. It was incredible, and I was grinning all the way home after doing eight laps of the park.

Now I'm considering whether I should change how I ride the race next week. In theory, riding at a lower cadence and in a harder gear means using more of my muscles to gain power. Conversely, a higher cadence and an easier gear offer less resistance to the legs; therefore riding is easier on the muscles but requires more cardio to get the same power. From what I've read, it's better to use a lower gear with higher cadence for triathlons because the leg muscles, and especially the quads, aren't so tired for the run. But my problem is that I don't seem to go as fast with a higher cadence and lower gear, so it might be worth considering riding in a higher gear but pushing the pedals slower.

When guys on faster triathlon-specific time-trial bikes pass me, I usually think that there's no point in me getting a faster TT bike since I won't be able to ride it fast enough. It will be a waste of machinery because the engine – namely, me – won't be big enough to power it. It's like having a Ferrari powered by a small Fiat engine; it will look sleek and fast, but it will be tortoise-like from lack of power. But after today's ride, I can see myself riding a fast TT bike and being fit enough to power it. Granted, it has taken seven months of constant training to get here, but now I see a way for me to achieve it.

Knowing that I could go faster is brilliant. It is just a shame that I experienced it a week before the race. Considering it some more, I think it would be better to stick to my original technique of higher cadence with easier gears. The Ironman is unknown territory; it's probably best to play it conservatively to ensure that I finish. The next time I ride my bike will be during the race, so it's probably not wise to start changing my style now.

With one week to go, I am starting to get butterflies in my stomach when I think about the race. I'm excited and nervous at the same time. At least it's reassuring to know that I've trained as best I could and that I'm getting faster and stronger. I hope that I'm ready.

Thursday, 20 July 2017

Well, this is it – I've done my last workout session before the big day. Today I did a 2,100-metre swim, which took just under fifty minutes. I concentrated mostly on my technique, still focusing on improving my breathing to my right. Two days ago, I did a shorter forty-minute swim, and I did the same thing then. It seems that my right-side breathing is improving slightly and becoming more relaxed. The other thing that I worked on today was sighting. I wanted to have steady rhythm when sighting and made sure that it didn't disrupt my alignment. It was hard to focus on individual points to improve my breathing, but what helped the most was when I slowed down my stroke rate, which allowed me to be more relaxed and in effect better aligned. It seemed counter-intuitive, but going slower might make me go faster. This is why swimming is so technical: because there is no point in powering away unless the technique is perfect. It is more efficient to focus on technique rather than flail my arms as fast as possible.

At the end of the session, I finished the swim with a pace of about 2:20/100m. From this, I estimated completion of the 3.8-kilometre Ironman swim in about ninety minutes. However, from experience, I know that my pool times don't quite translate to swimming in open water. There are a lot of factors in open water that can't be recreated in the pool, like the wind, choppier water and water temperature to name a few. Having said that, I feel ready for Sunday.

Yesterday, I did a twenty-minute run, and for some reason my stomach felt slightly funny. It was a weird feeling, and hard to describe. It seemed like I was hungry but not really, or kind of bloated with gas. It didn't hurt, but it wasn't normal. It persisted most of the day, but it seemed to have gone away today. Tania thought that it could be just nerves, and she was probably right. For a while, I thought it might be similar to what Elisa had last week, but it was hard to tell. She is back to normal now, so whatever was bothering her stomach seems to have gone away. I have to watch what I eat in the next couple of days as it would be a real shame if all my hard work goes down the drain due to a stomach bug or something. Fingers crossed I stay healthy and don't have any issues.

The first thing I've been doing all week after waking up is checking the weather forecast for Nottingham. Over the past few days, the long-term forecast has been updated to exactly what I've asked for: about 19°C and overcast. But unfortunately today it has changed, and it now looks like there will be rain as well for most of the day. That's not ideal for the bike ride, and hopefully the forecast will change again and it will be dry for the race. The other thing that I have to worry about is what to wear. With the cooler temperature, my tri suit might be slightly chilly, so this is something I need to think about to ensure that I will be comfortable and not too cold during the ride. With such a long day looming, I have to be completely prepared for any eventuality. We're leaving for Nottingham tomorrow, and I'll take some time tonight to inspect that all of my race kit is ready and that I don't forget anything.

Tomorrow is Sofia's last day of school before the summer holidays. A nice family trip to Nottingham for the weekend, to support her dad with the Ironman, would be an excellent start to her summer. It has been a long and exciting year for me so far, and I'm looking forward to after the race when I can finally take a break from training.

My Ironman journey has been nine years in the making. Something that was an impossible dream a few years ago is now within reach. I've come a long way, and this Sunday I look forward to chasing that smile and making my dream a reality.

Tuesday, 25 July 2017

The whole weekend was a blur, but I will aim to recall as much as possible. We drove up to Nottingham on Friday afternoon, and the whole family was excited. Sofia had finished school for the year, and so summer had officially begun. No more school runs for the next six weeks! Plus, it felt like we were going on a mini weekend break. However, as much as I would have liked to go out and do touristy things, I knew the weekend would be all about my race. I felt guilty we couldn't do much sightseeing, but I'll make it up to my family. Friday evening was pretty uneventful; we just had a meal after getting to the hotel, and then I went to sleep right away. I knew that I wouldn't get much the night before the race, so I tried to get as much rest as possible. Elisa woke me up at around 3am and then it was impossible for me to get back to sleep. My brain immediately switched on and started thinking about the race, and I couldn't switch it off. In the end, I got about five hours of shut-eye on Friday night, which was not ideal.

On Saturday, right after breakfast, we headed straight to the race venue: the National Water Sports Centre. I had to register and then attend a compulsory briefing before racking my bike in the transition area. I could have done a twenty-minute open-water practice too, but I skipped it since I wanted to at least spend some time with the girls. The registration went smoothly, and I was delighted to get a nice bag as part of my race pack. We also got instructions on how the transition areas are set up. The main difference with the Outlaw compared to all the other triathlons I'd done was that the athletes were given two transition bags: one for the swim-to-bike and another for the bike-to-run transition. We were required to get changed inside a large tent with all our kit inside the two bags; in contrast to the other triathlons that I've participated in, where normally our kit was set up by our bikes, and we got changed there. I supposed the Outlaw did it that way because some would prefer to wear proper bike clothes for the ride and then change into running clothes for the marathon, as opposed to using a tri suit throughout the whole day. With such a long day ahead, losing several minutes by getting changed into more comfortable clothes was better than being faster through the transition. I saw the logic in that, so when I packed my transition bags later in the evening, I put in my normal running clothes just in case.

After registration, I headed to the race briefing tent and started chatting to the person sat next to me. He was a young guy and my ears perked up when he told me that he was doing his very first triathlon. Most people would normally attempt the shorter distances first and gradually build up to an Ironman distance. But the kid looked confident, and told me that he'd attempted to do a sixty-mile ultramarathon last year but was unsuccessful, so the Outlaw would be his 'revenge'. I thought that perhaps his youth made him naive regarding the challenge we were facing, but I didn't say anything. I just wished him the best of luck, and then listened to the race briefing. The speaker reiterated that we had all done the hard work and should trust our training. That gave me a lot of comfort and confidence because I knew that I had trained as much as I could and hadn't missed many workout sessions. Assuming that my training plan did its job – which was to get me around the course – I should be fit enough to complete the race.

When the briefing finished I met up with Tania and the girls, and all I had to do was rack my bike in the transition area before we left the race venue. It was past noon, so we decided to check out some sights around Nottingham. That wasn't ideal, but I didn't want to suggest that we go back to the hotel to relax. We ended up visiting an old windmill that was still in use to make flour, which was pretty interesting. Then we went to the city centre and ended up getting a greasy burger for lunch. It wasn't exactly the best food to be eating before the race, but I let the girls choose where to eat, and I just followed. After we finished eating it started raining, and Sofia suggested we go back to the hotel and I happily agreed. We returned just in time to catch the end of the penultimate stage of the Tour de France on TV. I watched Chris Froome take the yellow jersey once again with a solid time trial; I was pleased since I had been following most of the Tour and cheering Froomey all the way.

I relaxed for a bit and then prepared my transition bags. My eyes lit up when I saw the temporary tattoos of our race number to put on our arms and calves. It was the first time I'd put on a race-number tattoo, and it made me feel like a pro. Once my bags were sorted, all that was left to do was eat and get some sleep. Since we'd had massive burgers and fries for lunch, we decided to buy something at the supermarket opposite the hotel as opposed to eating out again. It was a smart idea, and I got some pasta and salad, which was much better pre-race food than the greasy burger I'd had for lunch. Then it was straight to bed as I had set my alarm for 3.30am.

I had asked a fellow athlete who was staying at our hotel for a lift so that I could leave the car with Tania. The race started at 6am, and we had been advised to get to the venue by 4.30am. I aimed to get to sleep by 9pm so that I could have at least six hours, but I knew it would be difficult. My brain could not switch off, and pre-race nerves kept me awake. I wasn't sure what time I drifted off, but I woke up about three or four times during the night, and in the end, I beat my alarm and was fully awake by three. There was no point in going back to sleep, so I rolled out of bed and started getting ready. A number of athletes were staying at the hotel, so the restaurant was open by four and had breakfast ready for us. It was comforting to see other bleary-eyed athletes, and to chat with them to keep my nerves at bay. Soon after, Stuart – the man I had asked for a lift – came down and we were off to the race venue.

The drive was a blur, and we kept small talk to a minimum. We were both nervous, and talking about the race or our preparations probably wouldn't have helped settle the butterflies in our stomachs. I just stared out the car window and I thought about all the things I needed to do to get all my gear set up and ready for the long day ahead. I had gone over it all many times, so as soon as we reached the venue, I was on autopilot. It goes to show that visualising everything helps a lot with race preparation.

I rehearsed putting my transition bags on my designated hooks. Then I went to my bike to check the tyres, and put my bike computer on the bars, two water bottles in the cage, and all my gels and energy bars in a small bento box strapped to the frame. Then it was back to the transition to double-check my bags, and finally start getting my wetsuit on. It had been dark when we'd got to the venue, but by the time I put on my wetsuit and stepped out of the transition tent, dawn had broken. The tension in the air was palpable, and I was ready to get going. By 5.50am, we were allowed to jump in the water, and I picked the third dock to get in the rowing lake. It was supposed to be for swimmers who were aiming for around ninety minutes. I was hoping I could finish with my pack, but I would have been happy if I could get the swim done in under an hour and forty minutes. The water felt rather pleasant when I got in, and I did some practice strokes to help myself settle in and acclimatise to the water temperature. I then stopped and looked at the buoys in the distance. This was it: after seven months of training, I was finally starting my Ironman challenge. I'd made it to the start line, a tremendous accomplishment in itself. I smiled and had a moment. Soon after, the bullhorn blasted my ear, and the race was on!

I heed the race briefing advice and waited a few seconds after the gun to let the faster swimmers go ahead, but I was surrounded with about 1,200 other swimmers and I had no choice but to go with the flow. As I'd expected, the start of the swim was a melee, and it was like wrestling inside a washing machine. I saw bodies, arms, elbows and legs everywhere. I got kicked and dunked several times, and at one point I was completely on top of someone's back. But I managed to stay composed and relatively calm through most of this, even though someone was constantly hitting my leg. I breathed slowly and paid attention to my stroke. It helped a lot to keep my mind focused on something, and prevented it from wandering and thinking about the day ahead. At one point self-doubt started to creep in, and I feared that I couldn't finish the day. It was the worst thought to have in the middle of a swim, and it could have easily led me to panic. I pushed the thought away and concentrated on my stroke, breathing and sighting the next buoy. I anticipated for things to settle down, as normally I would be left swimming on my own at the back of the pack. But when I reached the halfway point, a lot of swimmers still surrounded me and I was still battling for space. I thought, *fantastic*, I was swimming with a pack and not on my own for a change, but it sucked to keep fighting for position. So I used it to my advantage and drafted behind someone. Just after the halfway point, I had a quick look at my watch to check my pace, and was confused when it said that I had only gone 150 metres! At first, I was worried that I hadn't made any progress at all, but then I saw that the timer didn't move, so it must've been accidentally turned off during the wrestling match. I quickly reset it and continued swimming.

The swim course was an out-and-back in the rowing lake and followed a rectangle that started and ended at the same point. As soon as I reached the third turning point, I knew that I was on my way home. My stroke was still consistent, but I was stalling a bit when I breathed to my right side. Since we were swimming in a clockwise direction, the shoreline was always on my left side. Hence, I decided that it was better just to keep breathing to my left in the last kilometre or so. I thought that I was sighting fairly well, and there were still a lot of people in front of me, so there was less risk of swimming in zigzags, even if I was just breathing on one side. That helped, and I was in a much better rhythm during the end of the swim. Towards the finish, I could see a lot of people had already started the bike ride as they zoomed past me on the shore. But I didn't let it deter me, and just focused on the finishing flags in the distance.

Fifteen metres… breathe, sight… ten metres… breathe, sight… I'm nearly there… five metres… I can see the rocks underwater… I can see the mats… I can stand up… I'm being helped out of the water. I've done it! I've completed the Ironman swim. I looked at the race clock and noted one hour and thirty-nine minutes. It was bang on my predicted time, and I gave a huge smile for the cameras.

When I got out of the water, they had strippers ready for me. Not the people who take off their clothes, but volunteers who helped us strip down our wetsuits. That was handy, as my wetsuit felt like it was glued to me, and it was a struggle to get it off. Even the strippers had a hard time with it, but eventually, after one or two good yanks, they managed it. Then I was off to the transition tent, and quickly found my bag. I didn't rush while getting my bike gear on, and made sure that I didn't forget anything. I was buzzing, and had a humongous smile. After a quick pee stop, I located my bike, and the next thing I knew, I was pedalling away from the first transition.

The start of the bike course consisted of a lap around the lake, which was wonderful. Looking at the massive distance that we'd just swum, it was hard to believe that I'd completed it. A huge sense of accomplishment rushed through me, and I laughed to myself as I shouted, "Go on, Howie – you're a legend!" I was having an awesome time, which was a brilliant start to the ride. As I rounded the top of the lake, I noticed that there were still a handful of swimmers in the water. The backmarker had just passed the turning point, and I calculated that he or she probably wouldn't make the cut-off time. I gave them a cheer anyway and then concentrated on pedalling. I settled into a rhythm and passed some people. Then I came across Stuart, the guy who'd given me a lift from the hotel. I asked him how his swim had gone and he said it was pretty bad to begin with. He'd had a panic attack, and turned around to start swimming back to shore, but once he was able to stand up, he'd caught his breath and managed to compose himself. He'd considered quitting, but after some deliberation, he convinced himself to start again and go for it. I was surprised when he told me, and it goes to show how hard a challenge it was for everyone, both mentally and physically. It reminded me that we all have our own hurdles to overcome throughout the day. I was glad that Stuart had managed to clear his first one, and wished that the rest of his day would go smoothly, and that I would have a good day too.

After our brief chat, I dropped back from Stuart since we were only supposed to ride in single file. Plus, there was no drafting allowed, so I had to stay at least ten metres behind. But then when the road kicked up, I ended up passing him, and then a short while later he passed me again. We played leapfrog for several kilometres until I realised that I was probably going too fast by staying with him, so I let him go and focused on my own pace. The course was fairly flat, so I was on my aerobars for most of the time. I kept my cadence between eighty and eighty-five rpm and was able to apply more power.

My only concern for the first hour on the bike was that my stomach felt bloated and I knew that it was gas. As much as I'd tried to relax and breathe calmly during the swim, I had swallowed some water and a lot of air. It had happened in all of my previous triathlons, so I was used to it. I had to get rid of the gas as fast as possible, not only to feel better but, more importantly, so that my stomach could process the gels that I was consuming. There was only one way to get rid of the gas, and that was by farting it out. I grinned as I recalled Anna's comment on my Facebook page the night before. She'd wished me luck and told me to make weird grunting noises like I'd made on our Kilimanjaro summit night when things got tough. I'd replied that I could also do acclimatisation farts for extra speed. I don't know if my speed got a boost, but some relief finally came after I took my first gel and a big, loud one came out. I just hoped that the person behind me was following the drafting rules; otherwise, they would've got a whiff of something awful. My ride-nutrition strategy was to take a gel every twenty minutes and an energy bar on the hour. After my first bar, I managed to fart all of the gas away, and I felt heaps better. Unfortunately, it wasn't the end of my stomach problems.

I cruised along for the first couple of hours, enjoying myself. I felt strong, and even managed to pass people. But then my stomach started feeling funny again. When I reached the third feed station, I decided to make another toilet stop. I was hesitant since I didn't want to lose time, but I reasoned that it was going to be a long day and toilet stops were inevitable. I was glad that

I did, because it was so much better when I got back in the saddle. Ultimately, I made three toilet stops during the ride, for a total of about nine minutes, which wasn't bad considering that I normally take much longer in the morning. Tania probably wished that I was racing every morning, because she always tells me that I take too long in the bathroom.

The bike course itself was fairly flat, with only one small hill around eighty kilometres into the ride. I was slightly apprehensive about that hill, but I knew I could tackle it. I'd studied the course profile, and it didn't look much harder than the climbs I'd been doing at Richmond Park. My apprehension was unwarranted as it was over before I even realised that I was climbing. I even had to ask someone if that was the climb, while cruising along. Afterwards, as I approached an intersection I saw Tania and the girls waving at me from the side of the road. I wasn't going too fast, so I had time to register that it was them cheering me on and not hallucinating. That gave me a boost and I easily cranked the pedals with a smile for the next hour.

About 150 kilometres into the ride, things got worse. It was as if someone had flicked a switch and the power disappeared from my legs. I wasn't sure if it was exhaustion or perhaps just boredom, but I felt a drop in power, and started getting tired. I then realised that I'd missed taking a gel or two, so I quickly took a couple to catch up. But it was too late. Even though I sensed a slight increase in energy afterwards, it was hard to get that focus back, and the last thirty kilometres was a real slog. I had to resort to my trick of breaking things down into little chunks to get through that last hour or so. Eventually, I rolled into the transition point after seven hours and twenty minutes. I was so relieved to get off the bike, and well within the cut-off time. The viewing stands were packed, and the cheer from the crowd lifted me up. It gave me another boost through transition, and then I was off to start the marathon.

After leaving the transition, I passed rows of porta-potties, and I considered making a stop. However, there were a lot of people cheering me on, and I was embarrassed going in, so I just continued running. The marathon course consisted of a lap of the rowing lake and then going out of the National Water Sports Centre and along the river to some point in the city; and then back again, making another loop around the lake and repeating the loop by the river. Finally, after returning to the lake for the second time, we had to do two more loops around it before crossing the finish line. Every 2.5 kilometres, I could look forward to an aid station handing out food and drinks.

When I started my first loop of the lake, I felt terrific, and maintained a decent pace. I grabbed some gels and just savoured the whole atmosphere. There was a big grin on my face when a motorcycle with a cameraman passed by me. I was startled, until a woman ran past and I realised that they were filming the leader of the women's race. I cheered her on, amazed that she was on her way to completing the race. Later, I read that she'd beaten the course record and finished with a time of nine hours and forty-four minutes. Even more remarkable was that, a year earlier, she'd been diagnosed with cancer and had undergone chemotherapy. The incredible power of the human spirit never ceases to astound me, and reading these stories always motivates me.

At the end of my first lake loop, I looked into the stands, where hundreds of supporters were cheering everybody. I then heard someone shouting my name, and turned to see my friend Alice waving at me. Her husband was also racing, and it was such an enormous boost to see a familiar face. As I passed the finishing chute, I was given a wristband so that I could keep track of how many laps I had done. I needed to collect all three before I could head to the finish line. It was fantastic getting the first one, and I made a date with the lady who was handing them out to see her two more times. As I rounded a corner, I spotted some porta-potties that were out of sight of the crowd, so I made a quick dash to relieve myself – and what a relief it was.

I then made my way to the river trail, where it was a lot quieter, though still busy, and I focused on maintaining a steady pace. It was a challenge not to get 'wristband envy'; it was really hard seeing that most of the people in front of me, and the ones coming back to the lake, already had two, meaning that they were on their second lap. I had to remind myself that I was running my own race and I'd finish when I finished. At that point, I started getting tired even though I had been taking my gels regularly and making sure that I drank enough. Without any spectators around to cheer or motivate me, I decided to walk a little. Part of the problem was that I didn't know how far away the turnaround point was, and it was disheartening. I tried walking for a minute and then running again, and I did that several times. Eventually, the course took me across the bridge over the River Trent and into a riverside park where Tania and the girls greeted me! It was such a thrill to see them, and to give them hugs and kisses. That part of the course was open to the public, and they could run with me for a while. Tania told me that my friend Kyle had posted the live athlete tracker on Facebook, and a lot of my friends were keeping track of my progress. It was encouraging to envisage all my friends from around the world cheering me on. I can't describe how wonderful it felt to see my family, and it gave me such a high that I picked up my pace. But then disaster struck.

The part of the course where I'd seen Tania was on a slope, and we were running across it. With each stride, my left leg was slightly more extended than my right due to the incline. Then a pain shot up from my left knee. I immediately stopped, then walked to shake it off. But when I started running again, the pain was still there. I started to worry when I looked at my watch and saw I was only ten kilometres into the run. I hadn't even reached the first turnaround point of the big loop. However, I told myself that there was still plenty of time, and focused on continuing. I experimented with different strides and some combination of shuffling and walking, which got me going for a while and eventually got me back to the lake. At that point, the number of athletes was starting to thin out because most had already finished. I was walking more and more and running less and less. It was quite demoralising to go around the lake knowing that I had another lap of the river trail to do, plus another two of the lake. Looking at my watch, I realised that I hadn't even done half of the marathon yet! I seriously contemplated calling it a day. Every time I tried to run, the pain in my knee got worse, and I didn't want to risk serious injury. I rationalised that I had done enough and there was no shame in not completing the race. But then I saw Tania, Sofia and Elisa, screaming my name and cheering me wildly. They could tell that I was hurting, but I gave them the biggest smile ever. I did a quick calculation and realised that, even if I walked most of the way, I would still have enough time to finish before the seventeen-hour cut-off. With great dismay, I resigned myself to walking, but I was determined to finish the race. When I left the lake for the second time to start the river trail again, there weren't many athletes left. Most of us who were still on the course were walking, and I found two other guys to walk with. But eventually I left them, as I thought it was better for me to try and walk/run on my own. I attempted a new technique whereby I ran for a count of thirty and then walked for the same time, and I managed to make some progress. The knee pain was still there, but I could endure it for thirty seconds at a time. I don't know how long I managed to do that, but eventually, another disaster struck. Each time I took a step, there was a distinct pain in my left foot. More worryingly, I was getting it even while walking. I stopped and did some stretches, but the pain wouldn't go away. I looked at my watch and realised that I still had about twelve kilometres to go. I was about to panic, but then told myself that there was nothing I could do; I just had to bear the pain and keep going. It was agony, and I was really worried that I might do permanent damage. But I tried to keep all the negative thoughts away and just focus on each step.

By the time I returned to the lake, it was getting dark. The spectators had thinned out, and it was lonely out there. The worst was that I still had to do two more laps of the lake before I could finish. It was demoralising, and the only thing that kept me going was knowing that I had enough time to make the cut-off. I had given up on my target time of between fourteen and fifteen hours; my only goal now was to make it to the finish line before 11pm. I was at my lowest point. The floodlights of the finish line were so tantalisingly close, and yet so far. Then my three angels came to the rescue again. I looked up to see Tania, Sofia and Elisa cheering, and they lifted my spirit back up. Sofia stepped onto the course and started walking beside me. I was nearly in tears when she told me that she would walk with me around the last lap of the lake. She said it with such determination, and I did not doubt that she could do it, so we said, "See you later," to Tania and Elisa and started the final lap. However, we were stopped by a race marshal, who told me that Sofia wasn't allowed to walk with me. I didn't have any energy to argue, but Sofia understood and told me it was okay; then she turned around and ran back to her mum.

I looked at my watch: 9.10pm. I set myself a new target of finishing before ten o'clock. Again, my family had given me the boost that I needed, and I was determined to finish in under sixteen hours. My personal best for my local five-kilometre Parkrun was twenty-three minutes and thirty-six seconds. I figured that I could walk five kilometres in under fifty minutes even if each step was agony. So I moved my arms and started swinging them for momentum. I picked up the pace, struggling to block out the pain. In the distance, I could hear Tania and the girls screaming encouragement. I visualised all my friends supporting me and cheering me to the finish. I kept my arms swinging and focused on fast walking until I rounded the far corner of the lake. I passed the car park where Stuart and I had parked over fifteen hours ago to start our day. It had been dark then, and it was dark now, but I could see the floodlit finish line up ahead. The excitement started to build, in equal measure with each painful step. Then I noticed the 'one kilometre to go' sign, and the girls came running up to me. Together, we would cover the rest of the course. I was walking fast as I knew that ten o'clock was fast approaching and it would be very close. Elisa struggled to keep up, and Sofia was practically running beside me. Tania picked up Elisa, and we were all side by side. *Five hundred metres to go; keep going, don't stop… four hundred metres; keep those arms swinging, ignore the pain… the finish is so close…* Then we were all on the red carpet, and Tania put Elisa down so that we could all run together, hand in hand. Tears flowed down my face as I released all the pain and emotion that I had been holding back for hours. The agony was immense, but the joy and elation were even greater as we raised our arms in triumph and crossed the finish line. I had done it! I am an Ironman!

The relief flooded in, and I had the biggest smile on my face. It was the most incredible feeling, crossing that line with my family. They had been part of every bit of my journey, and without them, I wouldn't have been able to chase my smile. All I could say was, "Life is good. Thank you, thank you, thank you… for everything!"

Crossing the finish line

EPILOGUE

After the Outlaw, I spent the following week hobbling due to my foot injury. Nonetheless, I revelled in the sense of accomplishment. I enjoyed the comments that my friends left on Facebook, and was humbled by compliments such as 'awe-inspiring' and 'your determination and perseverance are inspirational and borderline insane'. But at the same time, I was slightly disappointed with the race itself. Even though I was very happy to have finished it in fifteen hours and fifty six minutes, I was dissatisfied with the run. I knew that the finish time was not that important and the achievement was more valuable, but I wondered what my time would have been if I'd been able to run properly. Having said that, I knew that I wouldn't want to attempt another Ironman to find out any time soon. The training was such a huge commitment, not just for me but for the whole family, so it would be a while before I attempted the distance again. Despite my mixed emotions, my general mood was positive. I was happy and relieved that it was over, and looking forward to the rest of the summer.

My summer was amazing. It started with an awesome camping trip the weekend after the race. It was the beginning of my fitness's steady decline. I didn't care about what I ate, and I relished drinking alcohol once again. The following week, I flew to Canada and had an epic reunion with my best friends. Slater and I managed to organise a boys' trip to British Columbia, where we rented a houseboat and cruised around Shuswap Lake. Somehow, the six guys I'd travelled to Australia with made the trip happen; the Voltron force was united! Slater, Kyle, Andrew, Bruce, Roz and I, plus Jon (Slater's younger brother), all managed to convince our significant others to allow us a week off. The reunion was unbelievable, as I'd thought aligning all nine planets in the solar system would be far easier. I guess it was one of the perks of turning forty. The houseboat trip was so much fun, albeit tiring and not particularly healthy. We spent five days constantly eating and drinking, and, due to Canada relaxing its marijuana laws, I was also stoned for most of it. As much as I would have liked to practise some swimming in the lake, I did none. In fact, I had to use a floating noodle every time we jumped off the boat, to be sure I didn't drown. But I didn't care, because the trip wasn't about training for anything; it was about enjoying the company of my best friends, reliving our youth and looking forward to our forties.

After the boat trip, Slater, Jon and I continued the celebrations by going to a music festival called Shambhala. It was full-on and crazy. Three days of it was enough for me to lose any fitness I had left. But that didn't matter; it was an incredible experience and I was fortunate to hang out with Slater again. Even though it wasn't quite our birthdays yet, the trip was an epic way to celebrate turning forty, and our strong friendship. It will be hard to top, but we already have ideas for our fiftieths.

My awesome summer didn't end in Canada; it continued after I came back home. I spent a few days in London, and then Tania, the girls and I went on our summer holiday: two glorious weeks in Italy, Croatia and Slovenia. The only hiccup was that I was sick for the first three days; I guess my body had finally had enough after the Ironman and the week-long bender in Canada. Thankfully, I didn't have any more races planned, just two full weeks of pure relaxation on the beach. At that point I didn't care anymore about my fitness, and I indulged in all the delicious food and wine Italy had to offer, plus a daily dose of gelato. It was fabulous, and I didn't mind at all that I had gained three kilos by the time we came home.

Back in London, we only had a couple of days to return to normality. The girls started school soon after, and we were back to our busy lives. But the fun didn't stop for me. A week after we got back, it was finally my fortieth birthday. I didn't expect much since I felt that the whole year had been one gigantic present, but once again Tania astounded me by organising a wonderful and memorable weekend. She surprised me by driving us to Wales, where we stayed at a stately home that had been converted into a hotel. When we got there, the surprise continued as two of our friends and their families showed up. Then Tania and I, along with the two other dads, drove to a disused mine, where Tania had arranged for us to go on a deep-mine adventure. We put on harnesses and went down the abandoned slate mine, which was such a cool and unique experience. Now I can say that I have been both at the top of a mountain and deep below one. After that, we went back to the hotel and had a small party. The whole weekend was fantastic, and everybody had a terrific time. To top it off, I got a special card from Sofia which read:

Dear Daddy,

YOU'RE 40!!!
Some people may think that's old, but I think it's the right age for you!
This year, you've completed all your challenges and I'm very proud of you!
You've inspired me and taught me never to give up. Also, you taught me that you can do anything if you believe.

I love you so much, and I'm very lucky to have a dad like you! I hope you have a great birthday!

Lots of love,
Sofia xxx

After reading her card, my heart burst with love and emotion. I openly let the tears flow down. This year has been one of the best of my life, and I almost wish that I could turn forty every year! I am very blessed to have such great, wonderful, loving family, friends and kids, and a truly special wife.

I'm extremely grateful because most of the time I don't need to run a marathon, climb a mountain or do an Ironman to chase that smile. Most mornings, after Sofia and Elisa jump into our bed for our family cuddles, all I need to do is look at Tania, and that smile will be etched on my face to start the day. *Life is good. Thank you, thank you, thank you.*

I think Sofia is right: forty is the right age for me. But the thing she got wrong is that I haven't completed all of my challenges yet. There is one thing I haven't mentioned that I wanted to do this year, and that is to write a book…

Appendix A - Marathon Training Plan

Week	Monday	Tuesday	Wednesday	Thursday	Friday	Saturday	Sunday
1	Cross Train 40mins	Run in Zone2 40mins	Intervals 4x4mins, 90sec recovery	Cross Train 45mins	Rest Day	Run 45mins Cool down 10mins	Run in Zone2 75mins Cool down 10mins
2	Optional Yoga	Run in Zone2 45mins	Intervals 4x5mins, 90sec recovery	Run in Zone2 30mins	Rest Day	Intervals 4x5mins, 2mins recovery	Run in Zone2 90mins Cool down 10mins
3	Optional Yoga	Intervals 5x5mins, 90sec recovery	Run in Zone2 30mins	Run 45mins	Rest Day	Intervals 2x10mins, 2mins recovery	Run in Zone2 105mins Cool down 10mins
4	Optional Yoga	Intervals 3x8mins, 2mins recovery	Run in Zone2 30mins	Cross Training 40mins	Rest Day	Intervals 3x10mins, 2mins recovery	Run in Zone2 135mins Cool Down 10mins
5	Rest Day	Intervals 5x6mins, 90sec recovery	Run in Zone2 30mins	Cross Training 30mins	Rest Day	Intervals 6x5mins, 1min recovery	Run in Zone2 90mins Cool Down 10mins
6	Rest Day	Intervals 3x10mins, 2mins recovery	Run in Zone2 30mins	Intervals 5x3mins, 90sec recovery	Rest Day	Intervals 3x10mins, 90sec recovery	Run in Zone2 150mins Cool Down 10mins
7	Rest Day	Run in Zone2 30mins	Intervals 6x1km, 90sec recovery	Run in Zone2 40mins	Intervals 4x6mins, 90sec recovery	Rest Day	Run in Zone2 150mins Cool Down 10mins
8	Run in Zone2 30mins	Intervals 3x10mins, 90sec recovery	Cross Train 45mins	Run in Zone2 30mins	Intervals 6x1km, 90sec recovery	Rest Day	Run in Zone2 165mins Cool Down 10mins

Appendix A - Marathon Training Plan

9	Optional Yoga	Run in Zone2 45mins	Intervals 4x8mins, 2mins recovery	Run in Zone2 40mins	Rest Day	Run in Zone2 40mins	Run in Zone2 60mins Cool Down 10mins
10	Optional Yoga	Intervals 5x3mins, 90sec recovery	Run in Zone2 30mins	Run in Zone4 20mins	Rest Day	Run in Zone2 20mins	Half Marathon
11	Optional Yoga	Cross Training 45mins	Intervals 3x10mins, 2mins recovery	Run in Zone2 45mins	Rest Day	Run in Zone2 30mins	Run in Z2 150mins, in Z3 30mins Cool Down 10mins
12	Optional Yoga	Run in Zone2 45mins	Intervals 4x8mins, 2mins recovery	Optional Rest Day	Intervals 2mins, 1min recovery	Run in Zone2 30mins	Run in Z2 135mins, in Z3 45mins Cool Down 10mins
13	Rest Day	Intervals 6x 1km, 90 sec recovery	Cross Train 45mins	Run in Z2 25mins Run in Z4 20mins	Rest Day	Run in Zone2 30mins	Run in Z2 90mins, in Z3 60mins Cool Down 10mins
14	Optional Yoga	Run in Zone2 45mins	Intervals 4x8mins, 90sec recovery	Cross Train 45mins	Rest Day	Run in Zone2 40mins	Run in Z2 60mins, in Z3 60mins Cool Down 10mins
15	Rest Day	Intervals 6x5mins, 1min recovery	Cross Train 45mins	Run in Z2 25mins Run in Z4 25mins	Rest Day	Run in Zone2 30mins	Run in Z2 10mins, in Z3 50mins Cool Down 10mins
16	Rest Day	Intervals 2x5mins, 1min recovery	Rest Day	Run in Zone2 30mins	Rest Day	Run in Zone2 20mins	**RACE DAY!**

Appendix B - Ironman Training Plan

Week	Monday	Tuesday	Wednesday	Thursday	Friday	Saturday	Sunday
1	Swim 30mins	AM Turbo 55mins PM Swim 1hr	Run 1hr30mins	Swim 1hr10mins	Run 50mins	Bike 4hrs Run 15mins	Bike 2hrs
2	Swim 30mins	AM Turbo 55mins PM Swim 1hr	Run 1hr40mins	Swim 1hr20mins	Run 60mins	Bike 4hrs 30mins Run 30mins	Bike 2hrs
3	Swim 30mins	AM Turbo 45mins PM Swim 1hr	Run 1hr50mins	Swim 1hr30mins	Run 55mins	Bike 4hr45mins Run 40mins	Bike 2hrs
4	Rest Day	Swim 1hr	Run 1hr	Swim 1hr15mins	Rest Day	Bike 3hrs Run 20mins	Bike 2hrs
5	Swim 30mins	AM Turbo 55mins PM Swim 1hr	Run 25kms	Swim 3.4kms	Run 1hr	Bike 160kms Run 5kms	Bike 2hrs
6	Swim 30mins	AM Turbo 55mins PM Swim 1hr	Run 29kms	Swim 3.6kms	Run 1hr	Bike 130kms Run 6kms	Bike 2hrs

Appendix B - Ironman Training Plan

7	Swim 30mins	AM Turbo 55mins PM Swim 1hr	Run 32kms	Swim 4kms	Run 40mins	Bike 160kms Run 6kms	Bike 2hrs
8	Rest Day	Swim 1hr	Run 1hr	Swim 1hr15mins	Run 1hr	Bike 145kms Run 14kms	Rest Day
9	Swim 30mins	AM Turbo 45mins PM Swim 1hr	Run 1hr30mins	Swim 1hr10mins	Run 1hr	Bike 145kms Run 6kms	Bike 2hrs
10	Swim 30mins	AM Turbo 40mins PM Swim 1hr	Run 1hr10mins	Swim 1hr10mins	Run 40mins	Bike 3hrs 30mins Run 30mins	Bike 2hrs
11	Run 40mins	AM Turbo 35mins PM Swim 1hr	Run 30mins	Swim 1hr	Rest Day	Bike 2hrs	Bike 2hrs
12	Rest Day	Swim 30mins	Run 20mins	Swim 1hr15mins	Swim 20mins	Rest Day	**RACE DAY!**

ABOUT THE AUTHOR

Harold Cabrera was born in the Philippines, grew up in Winnipeg, Canada and lives in London, England. He currently works as a Software Developer and Data Scientist for Wise Traders where he develops stock trading systems. He spends most of his time with his family, plus running, cycling and swimming. Harold co-authored and published *C# for Java Programmers* (Syngress Publishing, 2002) to help Java developers learn the C# programming language.

To find out more, please visit:
www.chasethatsmile.com

This book is printed on paper from sustainable sources managed under the Forest Stewardship Council (FSC) scheme.

It has been printed in the UK to reduce transportation miles and their impact upon the environment.

For every new title that Matador publishes, we plant a tree to offset CO_2, partnering with the More Trees scheme.

For more about how Matador offsets its environmental impact, see www.troubador.co.uk/about/